# just use this mind

FOLLOW THE UNIVERSAL TRUTH TO ONENESS OF MIND, BODY AND SPIRIT

Venerable Master Miao Tsan

D1530817

**bright sky press**

HOUSTON, TEXAS

bright sky press
HOUSTON, TEXAS

2365 Rice Boulevard, Suite 202,
Houston, Texas 77005

Library of Congress Cataloging-in-Publication Data

Miao Tsan.
Just use this mind : following the essence of Zen to oneness of mind, body and spirit /
Venerable Master Miao Tsan.
p. cm.
ISBN 978-1-933979-90-8 (softcover)
1. Religious life—Zen Buddhism. I. Title.
BQ9286.2.J53 2010
294.3'444–dc22                                            2010028653

Original Zen poetry at chapter open and close © 2010 by Master Miao Tsan
Translated by Jay L. Gao and Chao-Hsui Chen in collaboration
with MasterWord Services, Inc.

10  9  8  7  6  5  4  3  2  1

Creative Direction, Ellen Cregan; Design, Wyn Bomar
Printed in China through Asia Pacific Offset

妙丰

Master Your Life.

Just Use This Mind.

# ACKNOWLEDGEMENTS

The author would like to acknowledge Jay Gao, Chao-Hsiu Chen, and Larry Payne for translating the manuscript from Chinese to English. Jay Gao translated the text and worked closely with the author and others involved in editing and production to ensure that the English text remains true to the original text and teachings. Chao-Hsiu Chen spent countless hours crosschecking the initial translation against the Chinese text for omissions and inaccuracies and offered many insightful suggestions. Larry Payne meticulously polished the initial draft that greatly improved the consistency in the expression of key concepts and terminologies.

A special acknowledgement goes to Ludmila and Alexandre Golovine for their generous support of this book and their tireless effort and enthusiasm. Their whole-hearted commitment to every aspect of this project makes this book possible.

Lucy Chambers and Cristina Adams edited the manuscript so that the essence of the message can be presented in accessible language to the general public. Ellen Cregan and Wyn Bomar brought their artistic touch to the layout and feel of the book. Kathleen Sullivan, Monica Danna, Laura Mayes, and Dasha Jitkoff Phillips helped develop approaches to publicize the message of this book through print and electronic media.

Special thanks goes to Jui-min Su and Jung-Wei Chen for making a great many helpful suggestions throughout the project and reviewing the manuscript. Fernando E. Delfin compiled the list of terms that became the basis of the glossary. Don McLaurin, Natascha Ostroumoff, Fernando E. Delfin, Larry Payne, Dasha Jitkoff Phillips, Wylie Phillips, Ludmila and Alexandre Golovine, Eric Sun, Heng-Yin Yang, David W. Lee, Frank Jen, Naishin Chang and many others offered invaluable suggestions during the editing process.

Finally, the author would like to thank his brother, Dr. Tien-Sheng Hsu, for his support in publishing the Chinese version of this book in Taiwan.

Shih, Miao Tsan

# TABLE OF CONTENTS

# FOREWORD
## Venerable Master Miao Tsan

The vast sky touches not the earth,

The bright moon illuminates the road Home,

Green are the mountains, white are the reeds —

Thou shall see the Collective for thyself.

This foreword opens not only this book, it also begins a new chapter in my journey as a spiritual teacher.

The following chapters present a systematic approach to understanding universal truth, based on my realization of the Mind's essential nature. This book attempts to clarify the apparent disparities among the Mahayana, Theravada and Vajrayana schools of Buddhism, and it demonstrates how all religions—expressions of different forms of withdrawal from dualism—have created practical challenges and even confrontations among their believers.

The book's key focus is to show the unique characteristics of different cultures and look deeply into the problems these differences have caused throughout human history in order to reveal a path toward resolution. It examines the validity of various religious and secular concepts and philosophies, with regard to impermanence, dependent origination, and the Mind. The core of this book is the description of the essence and functions of the Mind, and the primary underlying theme of the book is the universal truth.

The main purpose of writing this book and the motivation

behind my spiritual teaching is to discover the universal truth—the essence and functioning of the Mind—and reveal the path on which to actualize that truth through practice. My motivation to spread the dharma and the direction in which I engage with society at large both stem from this ongoing quest for discovery.

The formation of any system of understanding must have its own motivation and history. Let me share with you the journey that has brought me to this point in space and time.

As an aspiring spiritual seeker, I vowed to transcend the mundane world and eradicate all false views. Before committing to the monastic life, I was already deeply absorbed in Zen teachings—reading the records of dialogues of the ancient patriarchs, contemplating the truths in various koans, making many pilgrimages and eagerly seeking enlightenment. One day soon after entering my life as a lay Buddhist, it occurred to me that I should become a vegetarian. So the very next day, I became one. Another night, as I rested in bed, an inner voice called me to begin meditating. So that very night, I meditated.

During those days, my brother and I shared a bunk bed. We would often intensely debate philosophical ideas into the late hours of the night. Awakened from sleep, our mother would scold us to stop. "You two are always fighting like the warring gods, but what can you gain by winning, anyway? It's better that you get to sleep early—at least you'll get some rest!" Those debates strengthened our desire for the truth, just as they sowed the seed of my search for commonalities among different viewpoints.

In one such debate, my brother challenged me:

"Is it true that in Zen the unenlightened person is someone who does not know himself?"

"Yes," I replied.

Then he asked, "Are you enlightened yet?"

"No," I replied.

"Since you do not even know who you are, why do you believe so much in your own thinking?"

Hearing this, I was dumbfounded. I lost interest in all activities. I had suddenly been freed from all concerns except the lingering question in my mind. Looking down at my own fingers, I would often ask myself "Who is moving this hand?" and then, "Who am I?" Many nights I sat and cried until the late hours. My motivation to practice was gone, too. Just a few minutes would pass in meditation before that doubt would resurface. "If I don't even know who I am," I thought, "why meditate?" I would unfold my legs, but even that didn't make things right. "Who is the one that wants to unfold the legs, anyway?"

I felt stuck, with neither a way forward nor a way back. But I continued my pursuit of this path of enlightenment. Eventually, I came to the realization that the goal of this pursuit was letting go. It was the first turning point in my life.

Over strong objections from my family, I took the monastic vow so I could spread Buddhist teachings. Once I became a monk, I committed myself to a period of secluded retreat, a period of time which became another turning point in my life. As I delved deeply into the vast ocean of Buddhist teachings, I discovered many points of contention and contradictions throughout its history. Again I felt trapped and tormented by the disparities I found, and my fervent pleading to understand the truth caused me a great deal of stress, as well as physical and mental suffering.

Contemplating the history of Buddhism, I recognized that since the passing of the Buddha various systems had emerged to categorize his teachings. Even during the time of the great Indian saint Nagarjuna, controversies over these categorizations remained. Later, when Buddhism spread to China, new systems for categorizing the teachings again emerged, and the same thing occurred in Tibet. Time and time again, systems for categorizing and interpreting the teachings diverged from one another.

I firmly believed that because there is only one truth, the truth must be universal and consistent. But despite this inner conviction I wondered, "How can I, a mere individual, possibly have a chance of resolving long-standing historical conflicts among different schools and traditions?" I also questioned my ability to find the true common ground among all teachings. The disparity among the various schools of teachings mattered a great deal to me; I realized that I was not someone who could simply look the other way, ignoring the problems while continuing to put my faith in a single tradition's particular interpretation of the truth. I simply could not find peace by teaching students concepts whose validity I did not find convincing; however, at the same time I kept questioning my ability to unravel this great, historical burden among the schools.

This deep desire to seek the ultimate truth drove me to adopt the Zen teaching on the essence and function of the Mind as the basis of understanding. As I practiced, I compared divergent views of the teachings to the universal truths of impermanence, dependent origination, and the principle of causality and karma, as well as to the essence and function of the Mind, in order to find the common ground. I believed that this common ground could serve as the foundation of a spiritual practice that could resolve the apparent inconsistencies among various Buddhist teachings.

My attempts to find this ultimate truth led me to experience suffering on the mental and physical levels as severely as if I were a turtle attempting to leave the shell. Sometimes, I would sit or lay down in tears, hoping I could stop thinking because it was too painful. Sometimes I wished I could simply follow what I was told. I was convinced that the true path of cultivation was the realization of the nature of the Mind, but my attempts to resolve the inconsistencies between the Mahayana, Theravada and Vajrayana teachings still had a sense of urgency. I could not surrender until I had found the answer. I could not face myself without having that answer. Sometimes, my determination pushed me to the edge. I would literally beat my own head and body, trying to force the doubts back into my skull.

Once I knelt down in front of the altar, facing the Buddha and bodhisattva, and I vowed: "I give, without hesitation, my life for the true dharma. If my thoughts, my speech and the direction of my effort have been wrong, may the bodhisattva and dharma protectors let me die instantly so that I may not bring harm to sentient beings."

One of the realizations I had was that all teachings are manifestations of the shared karma of sentient beings. Accordingly, the system of categorizing the teachings is the result of the collective, shared karma. These systems, I thought, have emerged due to different karmic conditions, so any categorization of the teachings is really a categorization of the karma of sentient beings. Arguing over the relative aspects of these systems is akin to judging different karma as either right or wrong.

To be a southerner is not necessarily better than being a northeasterner, and the oriental is not necessarily inferior to the occidental. The karma of sentient beings is necessarily flawed, but there is no point in making comparisons in terms of who is the "ultimate" or the "best." In any case, the best karma in the human realm cannot transcend the state of ordinary beings. To pass judgment on karma is to miss the true purpose of spiritual practice, and an excess of theories only obstructs our movement toward liberation. The real spirit of Buddhism is to accomplish liberation from suffering for the benefit of ourselves and others.

Through the connection with dharma, I came to the United States several years ago to teach and train students in Zen. I had the opportunity to see firsthand the differences between Eastern and Western cultures, and I was able to perceive their respective shortcomings. In the process, I observed that many religious groups hold so tightly to their traditions that their attempts to spread a spiritual message end up creating more discrimination and biases than do the efforts of non-religious groups. This situation not only thwarts the original intent of their traditions, but it has also contributed to the emergence of wars and conflicts that have burdened humanity. And, ultimately, it casts doubt on the very purpose of religion.

Many Buddhist organizations have made a great deal of effort in Western society without significant progress. There are language differences, and there are also varying social values and ways of thinking—the cultural gap. Recognizing these barriers to understanding, I try to peel back the outer layers and packaging of the teachings. Once the packaging is removed, I can convey the concept of Buddhism to people of different cultural backgrounds. The purpose of dharma teaching is to solve practical human problems, not to transplant the burdens of cultural custom to people who do not share the same background. Ultimately, Buddhism must not propagate a particular culture or a tradition, it must lead us to the universal truth that benefits all beings. The universal truth has no exception; it exists regardless of ethnicity, history, geography, country and religion.

Using particular cultural traditions to share Buddhist teachings can encourage different people to interact, but the breadth of the message will be limited. Social values do not express the universal truth. Social value is a phenomena arising from the interdependence of reality. The only solution for all human conflicts arising from dualism is a principle that is universally true. And only a principle that is universally true can be widely propagated; all human beings should understand and adopt the universal truth as the guide for their actions and lives. This is my core belief, and my purpose as a teacher of the dharma.

Even after nearly twenty years as a monk, the pursuit of the truth remains in my heart. I still believe that truth has no exception and there is only one universal truth. Truth is the truth; it isn't merely a religious concept. Buddhism has a system of training that helps people realize the truth, but it is certainly not the only path. Truth is ever present, but it cannot be perceived without training oneself to set aside attachment. The most precious gift of the Zen teaching is the legacy of its training system and its clear, direct and concise presentation of the truth.

*The Awakened Self-Nature,*
*Primordially pure it is.*
*Just use this Mind,*
*Directly actualize Buddhahood.*

My goal here is to pierce the layers of confusion covering the truth. It is not some conventional wisdom of the street market. By sharing my inner journey in the quest for truth, I hope to spark your interest and share the understanding of these universal principles that have been revealed to me on my path.

Chen Zi-Fan said, "Since there are too many people to pay gratitude, one might as well thank Heaven instead." So, I suppose it is unnecessary to thank my brother. But to thank the Triple Jewels or my parents also seems too mundane, and it seems merely customary to thank everyone who made this all happen. Therefore, I might as well thank myself, the mountain monk.

**Shih, Miao Tsan**
Vairocana Zen Monastery, California

Others said so, I said too.

Pointing here and there, while the Moon is always bright.

Like the worn-out garment of Huang-Mei,

Superfluous once again, painting feet on the snake.

Grievance must have a culprit, debt its creditor,

Name-calling is quite unnecessary,

The green hills already have many corpses,

Beholding grudge in the Light, then came the Dust.

# INTRODUCTION

In the past, the traditional systems of culture, morality and religion have guided the thoughts and actions of each nation and region. Their frameworks provided restraints on negative behavior and goals that people spent lifetimes striving to accomplish. Since the eighteenth century and the dawn of the Industrial Age, the human race's desire for material gain has surged. This change in society's collective mentality and tendencies resulted in the rapid development of science and technology. Once that fundamental shift in consciousness occurred, the majority of people seeking understanding have focused on the external, dedicating themselves to exploring, pursuing and creating all manners of physical phenomena. This tendency to train only the scientific spirit has taught us to seek answers in phenomena outside ourselves. It divides the whole phenomena of life into isolated pieces, creating dualism.

Modern civilization's focus on technologies of every sort has resulted in a life that revolves around material objects and experiences that create sensory pleasure. As people become further attached to these pursuits, they seek and develop more and more sensual, materialistic, and fundamentally unstable phenomena. Because the mind that relies on these unstable phenomena is also unstable, the current culture that we find about us today is ever-changing, unsettled, and lacking in the knowledge of how to converge in oneness. We can call this bardo, or transitional, culture. When the instability of people's minds leads to the instability of phenomena, a wide variety of problems occur, including large-scale troubles such as natural disasters, wars and social disorders.

These difficulties make people doubt the stability of the material world and trigger in them the urge to find a path that will lead to the ultimate meaning of life, freedom from their distress and a sense of stability. Because modern man's thinking pattern is incompatible with the thinking patterns of the past, people today believe old systems no longer meet the needs of modern society. In their search for truth and freedom, today's seeker most frequently tries to emphasize individualism and the diversity of cultures, without understanding either the purpose of diversity or the foundation and feasibility of its practice.

While the old system of culture, morality and religion rapidly disintegrates, the new system is still in the process of being established. This process of deconstruction and re-construction has confused people. The establishment of a new system to replace the older framework is only a change in form, not in essence. Whether we speak of the past or the present, religious beliefs or secular mores, Man's true allegiance has always been his inner attachment —his instinctive belief in a separate independent self that exists in opposition to others and his environment. This self-centered thinking pattern is humanity's true religion, Man's inviolable sacred temple. When modern people reject traditional beliefs by adopting new religion or philosophy, they overlook the need for a true revolution of their inner religion.

To regain order and stability for the new world without falling into yet another dualistic framework, it is essential that we guide people to find the answer in their own hearts, rather than in their heart's comforting delusions. The answer is the universal truth that transcends all frameworks of space and time. Because it governs the evolution of phenomena, it can serve as the foundation of the new era of humanity.

The universal truth is the principle of creation. Each one of us has the ability to create our own reality. Whether we believe this ability is given by God or is inherent in the individual being, each of us utilizes this formless creative force to manifest a phenomenal reality around us.

This inherent formless creative force has unlimited potential, and the created phenomena can take on infinite diversity. But governing this infinite diversity of phenomena is the operating principle of this creative force. None of us can separate from our inherent creative force and its law of manifestation; none of us can live separately from the world we created. Every person's ideas, physical appearance, environment, relationships and all such phenomena are the specific manifestation of that person's own creation, and each one of us should take full responsibility for what we have created. In order to solve the problems manifested by our own creative force, we must take issue with how creative force is understood and utilized, not with the phenomena it has already created.

The creative force behind human life is dynamic because it continues to manifest new phenomena in each moment, yet it is also unchanging because the ability to create phenomena is always present. All phenomena are the embodiment of this formless creative force, but the phenomena themselves are not this creative force. Although the creative force within people is everywhere, it is without form or features. When we can achieve a thorough understanding of the nature of this creative force and make good use of it, we live with God: we are enlightened, and we practice the way of bodhisattva.

The understanding of this universal truth can provide a new way of living for the next generation of human beings. It has the potential to provide structures for civilizations, cultures and religions, based on wholeness and creative energy, rather than greed and destruction.

I put this understanding of the universal truth forward with the hope that all people—whether they believe in the old religions, cultures and moralities or not—will have the opportunity to understand and to live in accord with it; and that by living in accordance with the universal truth, they will find direction for civilization, re-establish pluralistic, open, stable, peaceful, unified and converged order in the new era, and elevate mankind from the current strife and pain of dualistic civilization to the abiding peace of unified civilization. The greatest human achievement in history is the ability to live in the light of the universal truth without attachment to form. Living this way is the only way to address the predicaments of human life, for today and for the future.

# 1   E M P T I N E S S   S P E A K I N G

Emptiness speaks, resounding far and wide,

Traceless and unseen, manifesting myriad existences;

Maitreya's arising like a rootless tree,

Lotus step each leading the way to Realization.


A thorough examination of the history of the world—of all the cultures, ethnicities, religions, nations and individuals—reveals many deeply rooted fundamental problems. But what escapes most people's attention is that the reason history always repeats itself is because the habitual pattern of human consciousness repeatedly opens the same doors in the lives of both groups and individuals. The pattern of problems in human life and a similar path of problems in the evolution of history lie behind these doors. The challenge that the individual experiences is the condensed expression of the greater societal challenge. Just as the changing color of a single leaf reveals the arrival of autumn, understanding the individual can lead to an understanding of the Collective. And, a true understanding of the Collective cannot be gained without an understanding of the individual.

Zen concepts provide a strong foundation for understanding and grappling with the issues confronting the individual in order to dissolve the dualistic delusions of the Collective. A true understanding of the nature of duality reveals the source of conflict within the individual as well as the origin of problems between social groups and nations. Once the root of an issue is identified, the next practical step is to identify what needs to be changed for us to attain happiness and ultimately the complete, eternal freedom of life.

Zen reveals to us that truth is the law that governs the evolution of life and existence. Without truth, there is no outlet for the problems of existence. Truth is without exception, unchanged by time, space, ethnicity, religion or any other factor. Truth is truth; it is universal, transcending every theory and philosophy.

## Habitual Thinking Opens the Mind's Doors

As our human minds continuously and unconsciously give rise to mind functioning, certain patterns emerge. These patterns channel our thinking in a particular, fixed direction. Once they become habitual, these patterns began to reinforce the very unconscious state of mind that generated the patterns in the first place. This lack of consciousness, combined with its ingrained mental habits, opens up certain "doors" in the mind.

Each instant of mind functioning can resonate with a set of corresponding phenomena, experiences and results through its connection with a certain "mental door." The reality we must confront and which defines the uniqueness of each of our lives is the consequence of these connections. Our habitual thinking opens similar mental doors, and going through them leads us in an endless loop back to the same set of problems and undesirable outcomes.

Our mental doors are modes of thinking, including concepts of right and wrong, self and others, judgments, opinions, beliefs, biases, habitual ways of mind functioning, even our religious beliefs.

The mind is formless but can encompass all, being endowed with infinite possibilities and malleability. Concept, opinion, personality, view and belief are all mental constructs that we consciously or unconsciously accumulate within the mind. Being surrounded by these accumulated mental constructs, a false sense of self then develops. The Buddhists call this self-attachment or attachment to "I," and each of us, seeking to become the master of his or her life, must surrender it.

Every mind function arises from the mind, and what manifests from these thoughts becomes the reality with which we must live. However, when we are facing a situation that we don't like, most of us fail to recognize it as a creation of our own unconscious mind functioning. Every stressful experience in our lives emerges from a mental door that we unconsciously but repeatedly open. Each of us is the sole creator of his or her own problems, and therefore we must face them alone. When we complain, we merely waste energy and life, which is precious. It is futile to complain, because problems will never disappear by themselves.

Encounters with certain people, for example, may tend to trigger confrontational interactions. While we can easily justify our dislike of another person, the real question worth asking is why does this person manifest in our reality in the first place? Why does his or her presence bring about such anxiety?

The truth is that a pattern of negative perception has taken root in our mind. Therefore, the mind automatically and unconsciously gives rise to mind functioning that connects the relationship with negative judgments and ideas. Not knowing the real source of the problem, it is easy for us to blame the other person to explain away our own uncomfortable feelings. In other words, the other person has become the problem. The same reaction and the validation of the beliefs behind it can be triggered time and time again, worsening the relationship and perpetuating the negative cycle of interaction.

We all judge our experiences through the filter of habitual thinking. In other words, we are unconsciously driven by how we think, and how we think determines the feelings and opinions we develop toward people, objects and situations. But such opinions and perceptions only distort reality, and unfortunately, humankind cannot help but interpret reality through self-centered thinking.

For example, when we find ourselves in an unsatisfactory situation, we feel angry. We can't help it. We characterize the experience as bad. Our direct, nearly instinctive reaction to such a situation is the result of the inconsistency—or the gap—between the reality we are confronting and our inner definition of that reality. The gap between the perceived truth and the actual truth causes us to lose our reference point and propels us into a stream of mind functioning which creates certain thoughts that build up as negative emotions. When we face a situation, we first create a thought to define that reality as "undesirable;" then we continue thinking more thoughts of dissatisfaction until they build into anger. The transition from a peaceful state of mind to anger is triggered by habitual, unconscious mind functioning.

But each thought we have also presents an opportunity for change, since every thought is independent and rootless, being empty in nature. Each thought arises and dissolves simultaneously.

Regardless of what the prior thought might have been, the potential for the next thought is unlimited: It can turn toward an infinite number of possible directions and destinations, because a free mind does not have to hold onto a particular trajectory in its thought-movement, nor do thoughts have to follow one another in a fixed pattern.

Only due to the habitual mental tendency does our mind functioning become set on a certain predetermined path. The so-called habitual tendency (or unconscious mode of mind functioning) refers to the fact that the mind becomes preoccupied by certain thoughts. When one of those thoughts appears, it necessarily triggers a set of corresponding reactions. We experience these reactions with strong inertia. Our habitual mental tendency is the direction our thoughts take when we don't consciously overcome this inertia to free them from the path of least resistance.

Uncontrollable reactions—especially anger, sadness or sensual indulgences—often become stubborn, nearly unstoppable attachments. It is as if we are an old phonograph record that keeps skipping at the same spot. Attachment is habitual thinking or an idea that occupies and disrupts our inner peace. When the mind becomes dependent on certain people and situations and repeats the same thoughts, it is attachment. When certain people, objects and situations continually bring out the same reactions and emotions in us, this is attachment. When we feel the urge to seek approval from a certain individual or take possession of certain objects, this too is attachment.

Various forms of attachment compel us to repeat thoughts and emotional responses that solidify the mental doors through which we perceive and judge the world. A life driven by attachment will be characterized by the repeated manifestation and deterioration of similar issues and problems. The root of these problems is always due to the inability to live according to the fundamental principle of creation. Everything in life is a manifestation of the Mind, and all phenomena are inseparable from the Mind. Without the Mind, neither phenomena nor creation can be established. This is the fundamental, universal principle of creation and life.

All sentient beings, whether enlightened or not, possess the mind that has the same capacity regardless of ethnicity, gender, socio-economic background, education, past or present. Since it is true that each being possesses a mind that operates according to the same universal principle of creation, why do we experience such drastic differences in our lives?

These differences exist because each of us creates, within our own mind, different patterns of functioning. These patterns form the "self" to which we become attached. Attachment is based on an incorrect view of the principle of life so it operates in opposition to life. All minds are equal in capacity and potential, but each of us creates different attachments or habits, and through these attachments different doors are opened.

All our experiences are the reflection of our mind's functioning. The process of life is the continuous experience of our own creation. Reality is the reflection of self-created thought, and accordingly we are the sole creator of our own lives.

Human beings hypnotize themselves unconsciously: Every

habitually created thought deepens our own belief. It solidifies the same door, the same experiences, the same relationships and the same issues, so that we live in a state of amnesia, a dream-like illusion.

Existence is, by nature, limitless. It cannot be separated from the Mind. The world created by the Mind is formed by our habitual tendencies and manifests itself in a wide range of occurrences. These varied occurrences interact and operate interdependently upon each other, producing a complex, intricately woven nature of existence. This state of existence is the "Realm of Flower Adornment." Within the world created by the Mind, countless factors have gathered over time and are on the verge of ripening. A single thought in the present moment can cause them to merge, giving birth to our present reality. Moment by moment, the reality of our life is created by the Mind.

No matter what happens in life, it is nothing but our own creation. We are directly and intimately connected to the existence resulting from our own mental activities; each of us creates our own reality, our life and the universe that we experience. A very important and profound concept in Zen Buddhism is that the Mind encompasses the Great Void, and all existence is the Self. Once we grasp this concept, we recognize that the power to shape our own life exists within us and always will. Life is the most profound learning experience, but we can only remove the obstructions and create a better, more fulfilling life when the right doors are open.

How do we live a complete, fulfilling life? First, we have to dissolve the habitually unconscious patterns of our mind functioning. In order to break away from these habits, we have to cultivate our inner awareness. Only by acknowledging what we're really thinking can we stop generating the repetitive, habitual thoughts that continue to open the same mental doors and cause us to experience the same phenomena.

Zen training helps us to eliminate the inertia of mental attachment. It breaks down the unconscious mode of mind functioning and restores the mind to its original state of purity, peace and clarity. A Zen practitioner must bear in mind that the goal of life is to actualize his original Pure Mind. This is the true guarantee of happiness and the key to complete freedom and nirvana.

People generally live by following unconscious thoughts and ideas. But how can thoughts and ideas that are unconscious lead us to the right path? They are just blind and deaf servants. But these servants seem to be all we have to guide our life's direction. We don't want to depend on them, but we have no other choice. This is mankind's dilemma.

All human beings attempt to make the world conform to their ideas, but at the same time we depend on our faulty ideas and limited experience to handle the problems in our lives. Because our attachment to these ideas causes confusion in a dualistic existence, most of us lead lives that are busy, chaotic and unsatisfying.

To move from this chaos toward freedom, the first thing we have to do is correct how we think and get rid of our attachment to our old, erroneous ideas. A Zen practitioner must replace false concepts with the right view of the truth, gain mastery over wandering thoughts and habits, and dedicate himself to training in his daily life. Once the confusion caused by the old mental habits is completely lifted and the true nature of the Mind is revealed, we can live our life according to the universal principle of life. When we live in this new way, we live as an *awakened one,* just like the Arahats, the bodhisattvas and the Buddhas, for the benefit of ourselves and of all beings—in every moment, through every thought and action.

A Zen practitioner needs to work hard to replace the old, unconscious view of reality with the right view taught by the enlightened masters. Practicing Zen can gradually teach you to recognize that all negativity in your life comes from your own thoughts and actions. You can learn to take responsibility for unpleasant experiences. Once you understand and can acknowledge that your present situation is the result of your past action, you naturally stop assigning blame to others for the suffering experienced in a dualistic world.

When you know yourself as the sole creator of your life's situations, you're better equipped to find the appropriate ways to deal with future interactions. This change in your thinking and approach prevents the repetition of problems. The Mind is both the entry to life as well as the exit for all our problems. So, to change our life and resolve our problems, we must start with the Mind—the source of all phenomena—by changing our thoughts.

Once you understand and can acknowledge that your present situation is the result of your past action, you naturally stop assigning blame to others.

## Dualistic Thoughts Lead to Conflict

In contrast to ancient times, the modern world enjoys a great abundance of resources in terms of cultural records and dialectic systems—ways to arrive logically at important truths. The development of religious thoughts flourishes in great diversity. But even though our era has the apparent advantage of knowledge, it has not been able to use it to find relief from the distressing conditions of human existence.

The explosion of technological conveniences has overloaded the world with sensory stimulations and materialistic pursuits that have blinded us to our true identity. Busy in the pursuit of a lifestyle of sensory indulgence, we have lost the mind's original purity and aroused countless new desires. When these are left unsatisfied, they lead to crime and social unrest.

Clearly, technology has brought both convenience and confusion to humankind. When faced with contradictions between the traditional religious and philosophical values and the reality of modern society, we get confused. Then, we challenge the contradictions. As the world around us changes rapidly, we begin to feel a sense of dissatisfaction with the flawed social, economic and political structure. And as new breeds of alternative religions and false philosophies emerge, they contribute further to our loss of faith and our inner confusion about the truth.

All signs indicate our lack of clarity about the direction of humanity's future. As we lose ethical standards and begin to feel a sense of purposelessness, we get more and more confused about the meaning of existence. At the same time, the proliferation of information and the idea of a "global village" have brought forth a crisis in the way the traditional social machinery operates and have triggered its gradual disintegration. Disturbances and uncertainties in the human psyche begin to manifest in the outer world through natural disasters and human tragedies; moral and ethical crises create social unrest. With this confusion as a background, emerging social values and ethics can't respond to the rapid pace of change, and we have clashing ideas among social groups. This conflict, confrontation, disintegration and reshuffling of our world order are ushering in a dark period of change for us.

These issues are not confined to one particular country, ethnic group or culture. What's going on matters intimately to every single one of us. Our welfare—our very livelihood—depends on us coming to grips with these concepts. Organized religion must recognize these shortcomings and guide humanity onto the right path. The results of our confusion cannot be avoided; it follows a universal principle that transcends race, politics, history and religion. It has no exception. The only path toward eternity is for us to live our lives according to the universal principle. Only a culture built on the same universal principle can avoid repeating the same dualistic conflicts of human history.

That universal principle is truth, something that human knowledge can never completely represent. Philosophies and religions are ways to convey the truth, but they don't constitute the truth. However, many organizations today value the truth as they see it, and hold the traditions they represent and protect above the universal truth. This approach causes enormous problems.

As these various organizations compete on the stage of non-truth, they try to monopolize their particular explanation of the truth, expressing their interpretation of it with contempt for one another. This self-centered understanding creates hostility between various groups of truth seekers and believers. All of them originally intended to liberate themselves through the truth, but they lost their way among the propaganda of truths, and they support their beliefs by engaging in spiritual war. Numerous religious organizations and their offshoots now find themselves trapped in this negative situation.

In the name of truth, they urge their followers to engage in the same activities, abandoning the truth and the welfare of their followers. But how can a mind of non-truth ever open the door of truth? No theory or spiritual figure—regardless of his or her level of realization—can convey anything higher than the truth. No speaker—or the ideas he expresses—can go beyond the scope of the truth. Any organization or self-proclaimed truth-teller that claims to be on par with the truth, or even above it, is engaging in the most extreme act of spiritual delusion.

Everyone is in possession of the Mind, which is formless but has unlimited capacity and creative potential. The different functions of the Mind can open up different doors in this unlimited field of potential. This concept is universally true.

The Zen patriarchs endeavored to reveal this truth by asking their disciples whether they could perceive Emptiness speaking. The Mind is as boundless as the Void. It is formless, but it can function in infinite ways. So, at this moment, can you hear

Emptiness speaking?

While the truth is formless like the Void, it can express its existence in any form. Therefore, truth does not have to be Christian—or specifically Catholic or Protestant—nor does it have to be Islamic or Buddhist. Truth does not have to be Theravada, Mahayana or Vajrayana Buddhism. Truth is simply the truth, and it is universal. Those who expound the truth are the real spokespersons of the universal truth. Only organizations and teachings that convey the truth can dissolve the conflict of humanity, and only when we are able to dissolve this conflict will we have a truly meaningful existence.

## Universal Principle, Eternal Law

In today's environment, religious doctrines are either too narrow or too broad in scope. Because they are out of scale with human experience, they can't integrate the material with the spiritual. Religion typically addresses the metaphysics in both the formless and the real; and the real has a distinct form. But many spiritual seekers tend to pursue just one aspect of the teaching that they follow. In focusing on just one aspect of the teaching, in separating the formless from that which has form, they defeat the original purpose of the teaching: withdrawal from a dualistic existence.

Spiritual and material realities should be integrated, harmonious, and mutually inseparable. When we favor one over the other, we deviate from the truth. Only a culture that harmoniously integrates spiritual and material aspects can survive over the long term.

With our excessive emphasis on technology, we have steered the value and purpose of human existence toward materialism.

Material phenomena—the creation of more and more things—can go on endlessly. And the results of pursuing and being dependent on analyzing and developing material goods has a destabilizing effect on the human mind. Technological pursuit, whose foundation is dualism, clearly cannot bring true peace of mind.

But when we focus narrowly on the spiritual realm, we are led into an empty definition of freedom that ignores real, concrete problems. Any spiritual practice that doesn't take the reality of human life into consideration will be in vain. Life is shaped by our personality; ignoring life's problems is the same as ignoring our personality and the karmic forces behind it. To ignore karma and the principle of causality is to confuse the branches for the roots. In the same way, any pursuit of worldly happiness or spiritual realization will fail.

The most important issue today is the over-emphasis of materialistic pursuits. Let me give you an example: The thought that brings about happiness originates inside of us, so we have, within ourselves, the natural ability to cultivate happiness. If we surrender our innate ability to be happy and instead rely on external factors for our satisfaction, we become passive participants in our life's environment. Living at the mercy of external events is a life of bondage, not freedom. Dependence on external phenomena for happiness is a form of passivity and delusion. Living this way gradually destroys the proactive creativity of the Mind, and dilutes the meaning and purpose of life.

The blind spot in human culture is the dualistic manner in which it conceives reality, the way we separate the worldly from the holy and the material from the spiritual. Philosophically, this way of understanding existence splits idealism—the Mind Only view—and materialism. But the highest Mind Only view must also be materialistic, and vice versa; phenomena and its essence must coexist.

The way the mind conceives, the pattern its thoughts follow, and the manner in which it functions (as concepts within the Mind Only view) still involve discussion of the material world—existence on the level of energy. Mental activity remains a form of existence and phenomenon, which are still functions of the Mind. So even pure materialism must also eventually find its way back to the Mind Only view, and the pure Mind Only view must ultimately integrate with materialism. Neither can exist independently.

The universal truth is the union of the Mind and phenomena, and consequently it is the right path for humanity. I'll put it another way: Humans created the materialistic world on the basis of spirituality, and it is through the materialistic world that the spiritual becomes complete. We find true spiritual fulfillment on the same path where we find material fulfillment.

Today's over-emphasis on technological development and materialism causes us to lose our life's focus. The microscopic, analytical approach stressed by technology-driven development is used to dissect the macroscopic, holistic nature of the Collective. As a result, our perspective on life narrows. Technological development is materialistic; it focuses on dualistic knowledge and creation.

Man's existence is also a kind of creation. Some religions attribute man's creation to God. But a critical—and often ignored—fact is that God is inseparable from humanity. The phenomena manifested by the essence are themselves expressions of the essence. Through functioning, the essence is revealed. Existence comes about through the Mind, and is inseparable from the Mind. In a similar way, the nature and potentiality of the essence are expressed through existence, so the Mind is also inseparable from existence. When we practice this principle of the unity of the Mind and phenomena, we practice according to the universal principle.

Buddhism, as a religion, expresses the truth in a certain way: neither outside nor above the truth. Only the truth is eternal, because it is universal and all-pervasive. The true purpose of all religions can only be discovered through an understanding of the universal truth. The core purpose of each religion is immortality, or the actualization of eternal existence. And immortality is the goal of human life, the ultimate meaning of human pursuit.

Eternal existence—that is, immortality—is the expression of non-duality. It is the complete integration of the relationships between the individual and the Collective. It is the harmony of spirituality and materialism, and it is the only approach we can use to resolve the conflicts in our world today. Immortality is our way of escaping the contradictions between the holy and the worldly.

The union of man with his Creator in Western religions; the oneness of Brahma and the self in Hinduism, the Wholeness of Heaven and Man in Confucianism; and the essential equality of the Mind, the Buddha and the sentient beings in Buddhism are all expressions of this eternal, non-dualistic existence of mind and matter, in the individual and in the Collective. The pursuit of these ideals marks the consummate development of human culture. History has no shortage of examples of sages who dedicated themselves to the actualization of this ideal, but few of today's philosophical schools have truly grasped what eternal existence means. And they have not found ways to correctly implement the practice that will achieve the goal of true immortality.

Look at it this way: If eternal existence is to be established, it must be based on a certain principle. Since the principle of eternal existence is the principle of the Creator, it must therefore be universal. This universal principle is the essence of the formless Creator, the law governing the phenomena manifested by the Creator. In other words, the only eternal existence is the universal principle.

When the individual's life becomes one with the life of the Collective, it is the attainment of immortality, the highest actualization of that person's potential and completeness with the Collective. This union makes the perfect liberation of the individual and nirvana possible; it is the transcendence of the creation and destruction of the Collective. The interplay and union of the individual and the Collective happen in the present, moment by moment.

Immortality is not something that can only occur in the future, after the death of our physical body. When we realize that we are both the Collective and a part of the Collective, this is the union. It is the beginning of immortality.

Enlightenment, as taught in Zen, means that through every

moment of change we remain in recognition of our oneness with the Collective. Each of us is both the Collective and a part of the Collective. When we have this awakening, we can understand that the individual is the Collective and the Collective is the individual. They are inseparable and indistinguishable.

All religions and philosophies attribute necessary characteristics to the universal principle—the Creator, eternal existence or primordial nature. These characteristics are formlessness, omnipresence, omniscience; they transcend time and space and are able to create and encompass all. The Creator—or the universal principle—represents eternal life, the completeness of the Collective. By understanding and living according to this universal principle, we can create changes in every moment of our lives. Changes made through this universal principle allow us to attain complete freedom.

We can achieve immortality, but first we must let go of the attachment we have developed during the impermanent, brief existence of our individual selves. Phenomena are always in a constant state of flux. To grasp any impermanent phenomenon is to act against the eternal nature of the essence of life.

Instead, we must grasp the ever-changing functioning that arises from the essence of life. Our existence is not permanent because it must obey the law of impermanence. If we place hope for immortality in a future phenomenon, we are bound to face the cruel reality: The future, like the present, cannot escape dissolution.

All that is created is impermanent. Whether it is in some distant future, in a certain Pureland or in a heavenly abode, it is governed by the law of all phenomena: arising, abiding, deteriorating, and disappearing. However, the eternity of life is certain because it is the primordial nature of the Mind. It is the ever-present light of the unchanging, and the essence of all phenomena. Only that which has the nature of eternity can manifest eternity; other than that, no amount of effort can accomplish it.

The essence of phenomena is the entirety of life, our true refuge. The union with the Creator is true immortality; the oneness of the mundane and the spiritual is the true immortality. The universal principle manifests itself in the individual who is united with the Collective.

For the individual, this union is the liberation, the awakening; for the Collective, this union is nirvana. Eternal existence will always be the ultimate goal for humanity. It can only be fulfilled through the non-dualistic union of the individual and the Collective, which is the universal principle of Mind and Matter.

## The Immortal Door of Liberation

Buddhism originated three thousand years ago in ancient India. Its founder was a prince known as Siddhartha Gautama. He attained the state of Buddhahood through diligent practice as a monastic and was respectfully known as Sakyamuni Buddha, or simply the Buddha. Sakyamuni Buddha's enlightenment was not only a historical event, but it also served as an example for all beings.

The Buddha taught us that all beings possess the "Buddha nature." He revealed the truth that the Mind that does not separate the mundane from the spiritual is the essence and source of life.

His teaching is no different than the message of the Zen patriarchs: Through diligent practice, all beings can attain enlightenment and liberation, or the state of Buddhahood.

The Buddha remains a pioneer of enlightenment in our recorded history. The Awakened One taught the universal truth of the nature of the Mind: causality, dependent origination and impermanence. He showed sentient beings how to attain realization, completely eliminate suffering, and achieve true happiness by freeing themselves from the cycle of reincarnation.

The term "Buddha," in the context of Zen, refers to the primordially pure Mind. The Pure Mind is the origin and source of all existence. We all possess a mind, and it can, whether pure or filled with attachments, manifest various phenomena. The Mind is all-encompassing, omnipotent, omniscient, eternal and formless. It is the source of life, the Creator of all existence in the universe.

The essence of Zen practice is the non-dualistic union of mind and matter. Zen practice uses a system of methods developed over an extensive history of teaching and training experiences. It is designed to eliminate dualistic thinking and attachments. Through this system of training methods—which is, of course, not the only approach—we can dissolve the fundamental ignorance of truth, return and merge with the life of the Collective, and fulfill the pursuit of eternal life.

Among the world's cultural traditions, Zen is considered the practice of wisdom, the knowledge of the universal principle and life. The spirit of Zen teaching is held in great regard by people of various cultures and ethnic traditions. The practice of Zen brings about a positive influence on the individual, and also improves his interaction with the environment. Zen practice improves life here and now, and eventually leads to the attainment of freedom from worry and a deep sense of abiding joy.

The key idea in Zen is "Mind Only." All situations we experience, whether we choose them or not, are manifested by the doors we have opened in the mind. All situations and problems encountered in life are caused by the doors that were created in the mind, because the phenomena that occurred developed as a response to these doors being opened. Because of this relationship between our reality and our mental doors, we should not confront the surface of a problem. Instead, we should take personal responsibility and correct the underlying pattern of thinking that has created the problem. Every problem that manifests in our life is simply a reflection of our inner problems.

Enlightenment has a special meaning for the Zen practitioner. It represents freedom, the union and integration of the individual with the Collective, the discovery of the true point of reference and actualization of eternal life, and the manifestation of the universal principle in one's life. In other words, it is the starting point of nirvana: the unborn, undestroyed state of liberation in Buddhism.

Enlightenment occurs when we break down the unconscious, habitual thought patterns that have become attached to the Mind. It occurs when we break down the delusions we have about our selfhood and the confusions about the relationship of the spiritual and the mundane that our delusion of independence has caused. And it occurs when we live according to the universal principle, the truth. In other words, enlightenment is the primordial purity of the Mind, a state in which "self" has no meaning except as a reflection of the Collective.

The concept of enlightenment is clear and precise in Zen. It is beyond relativism and above the level of dualistic thoughts and discussions. Without the true realization of the nature of Mind, any amount of knowledge or the most detailed description will be nothing more than the chattering of relativism. We can only realize the true principle of the universe and human life by attaining enlightenment to the nature of the Mind, so enlightenment is the goal of every Zen practitioner.

According to the Buddha's teaching, even the heavenly realms or the Purelands of the Buddhas are subject to arising, abiding, deterioration and dissolution. The Western Land of Bliss of Amida Buddha will someday dissolve, the *samboghakaya* of Amida Buddha will enter *parinirvana*, and *Avalokiteshvara*—the bodhisattva of Compassion—will succeed and continue as the world's teacher. So where will Amida Buddha go after parinirvana?

Many Buddhists aspire to be reborn in the Land of Bliss, but what would it be like after the inevitable dissolution? For many practitioners, the Land of Bliss is a guarantee, a refuge, for the attainment of eternal life. The prospect that even the Land of Bliss is subject to dissolution is a source of confusion and anxiety for them.

We must recognize that the attainment of Buddhahood—or just the rebirth in the Land of Bliss—is not life's ultimate goal. Life is subject to ceaseless change. We cannot stop it from happening because change (or impermanence) is a universal principle. Ultimately, the samboghakaya and *nirmanakaya* (the transformation body) of the Buddhas will dissolve, which is why even after the creation of the Purelands the Buddhas continue to return to this world of suffering in order to liberate sentient beings.

In the Agama Sutras, there is a case in which the Buddha's disciples asked him about what happens when a practitioner attains *arahantship*, or the state of permanent liberation from the cyclical existence of the six realms. The Buddha responded to the disciples that after attaining arahantship one should continue to learn what has not yet been learned and attain what has not yet been attained.

Because the reality around us changes constantly, true liberation is the ability to remain in a state of complete freedom in the midst of impermanence. It is the ability to live in this changing world from an unchanging *oneness of mind and matter.* In this state of oneness, we find peace and joy.

Change causes panic and confusion for ordinary beings. In an attempt to regain and maintain a delusory sense of stability and existence, which they cherish as "I," they grasp for control of the situations that surround them. But evolved beings are able to rest in profound peace amid change, manifesting the universal principles and the innate purity of the Mind. Because evolved beings have eradicated the false "I," they are able to reunite with the Collective, free of any sense of separation in their material and spiritual lives.

Everything that happens is impermanent, so immortality cannot be established upon any phenomenon in space and time. The only eternal property of the existence we experience is ceaseless change.

In other words, the eternity founded on the nature of the Mind is the true eternity. That eternity is the ability to continuously create, manifest, and encompass phenomena from the Mind's primordial nature. The innate emptiness of the Mind—its ability to manifest everything that happens but not be bound by any of it—is the eternity of the Mind's essence. In a similar way, the Mind's limitless capacity to create and manifest all forms of existence, such as the unlimited capacity and potential for creation, is eternal. And this eternity is the eternity of the functioning of the Mind.

The principle of eternity is the union of mind and matter. Each moment of creation arising from the Mind is neither nothingness nor existence. It is what Zen called "truth as it stands" or "suchness." The moment of creation is exactly where truth stands. In the instant we have a thought, the essence of the Mind gives rise to changes in how it functions in response to the various factors in time and space that are brought together and interwoven with all the changes in reality already encompassed within the essence of the Mind. The changes brought about by the new thought and the changes already in progress reflect off each other. Together, they affect the myriad layers of reality, in all its various spatial and temporal dimensions.

Because the primordial nature of the Mind transcends space and time, the essence and function arising from this primordial nature transcend space and time as well. The essence of the primordial nature manifests the existence of the Mind, and the function of the primordial nature can create an endless range of situations and phenomena. When we truly realize this principle, out of the primordial nature, we can create phenomenal changes. These changes can occur through various causes and conditions, and we can enjoy complete freedom from any subject-object or space-time duality. This freedom is possible because there is no attachment to "I."

The limitations of space and time necessarily lead to cyclical existence. Evolved beings change phenomena out of the pure nature of the Mind, which is not bound by space and time. Space and time are illusions arising from attachment to the self, or "I," the attachment which prevents ordinary beings from realizing the Pure Mind. The Pure Mind functions and manifests phenomena moment to moment. As stated in the Diamond Sutra, it "manifests without abiding." To function through the formless primordial nature of the Mind is liberation, the display of universal principle and the ultimate evolutionary path for humanity.

Reducing existence to its simplest level is materialism, and taking nonexistence to its extreme is Mind Only. But, in truth, both materialism and Mind Only are inseparable from the unity of mind and matter. Zen's "truth as it stands," philosophy's "unity of mind and matter," religion's "union of man and God (Heaven, Brahma)" and Buddhism's "all beings possesses Buddha nature" are all concepts of this inseparable union, this non-duality.

Non-duality should be the direction of human evolution, but this goal cannot be achieved without both a correct understanding of what it means and an appropriate way to apply that understanding. Throughout history, many philosophical schools and religions have expounded the concept of non-duality. But, the over-emphasis on restraining dualism or the eagerness to invoke faith in men, tend to result either in objectifying or anthropomorphizing the formless, non-dualistic principle. Both these tendencies make the serious mistake of creating mutual exclusivity.

A spiritual refuge based on a tangible, knowable representation of a non-dualistic principle cannot be universal; by nature, it is other-rejecting. Such a spiritual concept is only a belief, not the truth. Furthermore, spiritual refuge based on an objectified or anthropomorphic representation of the truth is inherently contradictory to the non-dualistic principle, both in theory and in practice.

We cannot base our withdrawal into non-duality on the denial of the individual. Instead, we need to seek a withdrawal that completes the Collective through the individual. Here, the individual takes the Collective as its essence, while the Collective functions through the individual. Any approach to the non-dualistic principle based on the negation of the individual is both impractical and incorrect.

Anthropomorphic presentation of the non-dualistic principle is not universal; any theory or reality that is other-rejecting is neither the true refuge nor a feasible solution for human conflicts. In fact, such an approach can only deepen the schisms and fighting among social groups, because the attempt to give a physical form to the non-dual principle is essentially dualistic. Because it is other-rejecting, it is a source of conflict.

Only a religion that is based on the universal principle and has the breadth of teaching to integrate other spiritual principles can restrain and eliminate human conflict. The universal principle is the highest principle of the universe; ordinary spiritual concepts and cultures are very limited by comparison; they are like small lamps in the Great Void. Most philosophical ideas or familiar conceptions of non-duality are not only impossible to actualize through practice, but, in fact, they deviate from the universal principle.

Many religions and philosophies today encourage their followers to aspire toward rebirth in certain heavenly realms or Purelands. Zen practitioners, on the other hand, aim toward enlightenment as the realization of the primordial nature of the Mind. They strive to "return home," home being our original, primordial nature. When our consciousness is free of the delusory self and can reunite with the wholeness of the Pure Mind, there is no more "I" to be found. The concept of "I" is based on illusion. It wrongly takes thought as the self. This self-attachment insists on the existence of an unchanging entity that is the "I." This "I" is utterly false. In fact, this concept of "I" is the greatest delusion of mankind.

For the awakened ones who have returned home, the real "I" is nothing other than the Pure Mind. Finding the Pure Mind, we find the true self; and in finding home we meet the true Creator of life. The individual who is able to function from the Pure Mind and in freedom from delusions and attachments lives fully, having a completely free will. This is the meaning of liberation.

The term "Buddha" refers to the Pure Mind we all possess. The ultimate goal of meditation is to realize this Pure Mind according to the universal principle, and to perfectly and completely manifest Buddhahood. In turn, Buddhahood is the absolute wholeness and eternity of life. Zen practice is intended for the purpose of awakening one's own innate Buddha, purifying the mind in order to attain the manifestation of Buddhahood. It is neither possible nor necessary to become Sakyamuni Buddha. Everyone possesses a mind that is primordially pure in essence, so simply removing the egotistical "I" is enough to reveal its innate purity.

The manifestation of the Pure Mind is the basis of Buddhahood; it is also the point where mind-matter non-duality occurs. At the level of essence, the ability of an ordinary person's mind is no different from the Buddha. At this level, an ordinary person has the opportunity to recognize the nature of the Mind and live according to the universal principle.

When we are able to merge with the Collective of existence in every moment of change—in other words, when we, as functioning individuals, awaken—we are the Collective, and therefore the Collective is inseparable from each one of us. The state in which we intermingle with the Collective, living and functioning and feeling the oneness of mind and matter, is eternal life. This is the liberation beyond birth and death.

The purpose of Zen training is to return us to our true home— our primordial nature, the Pure Mind where life is eternal and mind and matter are one. Only in this true home can we become the master of our own mind and thoughts. Subduing our habitual, wandering thoughts and letting go of our attachment to worldly things and events requires diligent practice. When we are finally able to arrive at our true home, we directly experience the unity of mind, body and the environment. We are freed from separation and distinctions. This is the manifestation of the true self, or the real face of life.

This is a profound truth: "*Each drop of water contains the taste of all water; every moment contains the sign of all existence.*" All Zen practitioners should focus on training the mind from moment to moment in order to eradicate the unconscious pattern of mind functioning and self-attachment. The Mind already possesses all the wisdom.

For those who practice it, meditation is a means by which attachments can be transformed to bring about a peaceful, harmonious life and relationships. The most concrete way to apply Zen training to our lives is to correctly use meditation to transform the our habitual, delusory thoughts and bring that heightened level of awareness into our daily life. The method taught in Zen clearly points out the path to true freedom. It is very effective in clarifying the core of life's issues and changing the course of life so that we can be liberated from the cyclical existence of the false "I."

Sakyamuni Buddha revealed the immortal, right view of the non-dualistic union of impermanent phenomena with the nature of the Mind. He explained the true meaning of the oneness between the Mind (or the Creator) and the phenomena (or the created) in every moment. The Buddha handed humanity the right map, the universal truth of life. The teachings recorded in the scriptures are doorways to liberation, and he opened these portals for all humankind.

Hopefully, as you read and begin internalizing these concepts, you will begin the journey of letting go of the burden and attachment to this illusion-like self. You will shed the habitual, phenome-non-grasping tendencies that cling to your mind, and you will begin moving toward a new door, a door of liberation and fulfillment. No matter how far the destination is, Sakyamuni Buddha and all the enlightened sages have shown that ultimately you will arrive there. As you read further, you will obtain the map and the keys needed to find and reach the door of immortality.

Holding up a flower, the Buddha's scriptures are not used,

Facing the wall of the Mind, all future births cease forever;

Where can the descendant of the Patriarchs be found?

Seeing through the Void, the Moon is thus Luminous.

# 2 THE SEAL OF DHARMA IS NOT OBTAINED FROM OTHERS

Who is seeing, who is listening, who is talking,

Spring flower, spring breeze, the Spirit's beauty;

Not blind, not deaf, nor speechless,

No eye, no ears, yet wondrous in many ways.

The attainment of the universal truth requires that we first understand the indivisibility of the most basic relationship between the individual and the Collective. Every momentary change in our lives is a microscopic reflection of the functioning of the Collective in the here and now, because we are part of the Collective. The attachment to the false sense of concrete, independent individuality—a reality which in fact changes with each moment—prevents us from recognizing our true oneness with the Collective. The individual and the Collective are indivisible. Our attachment to the sense of independent selfhood, and the confusion it causes, is built on the false understanding that our thoughts are ourselves. This sense of identity as separate from the Collective prevents us from merging with the Collective and keeps us in a state of duality.

In other words, the false sense of independent selfhood and all its accompanying illusions have caused a state of conflict and contradiction for the phenomena presented by the Collective. When the individual is trapped by the confusion of the phenomena of the Collective and is unable to bridge the gap with the Collective through inward illumination of the source of duality, he will inevitably go against himself. Suffering is the inevitable result. Freedom from suffering can only come with the right view: we must train to break through the false sense of self that is developed from habitual grasping and the attachment to our thoughts.

## The Mirror's Reflection Reveals the Root Cause of the Problem

The Collective is the primordial nature of the Mind and all it encompasses; the individual is the momentary existence of the Mind's functions and manifestations. In life, man has already suffered for a long time due to his own mental habits, becoming lost within the karmic ocean of the Mind's collective essence. For those who seek to experience the merging of the individual with the nature of the Mind and find release from the confusions of dualism to manifest the universal principle, preparation for adopting the proper attitude and right view is very important.

Many spiritual seekers and believers, whether newcomers or veterans, think they are ready to create a better life through faith and practice. But the reality may be to the contrary. Life is like a battlefield of individual effort, so you must ask yourself: Are you ready to defeat your attachments? Those who feel ready are like soldiers who march into a war zone with their weapons. But the possession of weaponry does not mean you are adequately prepared—it does not guarantee that you know how to use the weapon properly, nor does it imply any ability to properly handle the various situations that might arise. Even if you have been involved with spiritual practice or a religious group for a long time, your readiness does not guarantee victory.

The true meaning of spiritual readiness is the willingness to face your own problem—the real problem in life—and ultimately its source in the mind. The unity of essence and function is the truth, which is universal. The person who is ready to make a change has recognized this view, knowing that the only true path is to take everything that happens as a manifestation of the mind and look back to the essence of the situation, instead of trying to make or prevent things from happening.

All phenomena are created by the mind. When we take certain thoughts created by the mind to be "I" and use this "I" to grasp or reject the phenomena created by the same mind, we make a mistake. That mistake is due to our ignorance of the truth. Lamenting the never-ending road of inner conflict, it was once said, *"Born out of the same root, why pit one against another so eagerly?"* This approach is similar to a person deludedly using his right hand to reject his left hand, not knowing they are both part of his body. If we can break through the deluded attachment to phenomena and instead recognize their essence, both we and the phenomena will be liberated as they are. When we are able to make this break, we—and the Collective—become an integral part of the wholeness of primordial nature. This is oneness.

The Tathagata attained awakening by working through obstacles. The presence of difficulties in life shows that the way of attachments has reached a dead end. We must face our obstacles and reflect inwardly, deeply contemplating the reality of our so-called problems or obstacles. We must be able to skillfully change our own thoughts as we guide ourselves out of the current predicament.

There is a Zen saying that "*the answer is in the question.*" The answer will present itself when there is a true understanding of the root of the question. Recognition of the root cause of a problem is the only way to alleviate suffering. Knowing the Mind to be the source of all questions and answers is vital to transcending duality and its myriad complications.

Because the individual has mistakenly established the perception of an independent existence apart from the Collective, the clash that emerges from this separation is the root of all obstacles. The complete union of the individual and the Collective is the only path to resolution. When we encounter problems, we must first acknowledge the problem and then be willing to face it squarely. Facing a problem means seeing oneself as the sole creator of the problem and as the one experiencing the problem in the present moment. Knowing scriptures or hearing the truth is not enough to truly own this fact. It is a profound realization, a realization from the depth of our heart, that we have been the lead actor in our life's dramatic play of happiness, sadness, union and separation. This life we experience is only our own.

A problem does not originate from outside of us. If we fail to understand this truth and instead insist on delegating responsibility outside ourselves—creating blame—we have not been properly prepared to uplift ourselves spiritually. And as long as we fail to understand this truth, we will not find any true success in life. To be blind to the root of a problem is to be a soldier who does not know the whereabouts of his enemy. A problem cannot be resolved unless we know its cause; unless we are able to shoulder the responsibility for self-reflection, we will miss the opportunity for change.

We are fooling ourselves if we believe that all responsibility lies in the external circumstances and deny that the issue is us, that we are the enemy. By failing to distinguish the friend and the foe, we have no chance of changing the reality. Instead, we will become immersed in a firefight of blame between ourselves and others. We will live a restless and frustrating life of futile depression. In the poem *Awakening the World*, Lo, who achieved first place in the imperial examination, wrote:

> *Restless and hurried man pursues in suffering,*
> *cold and warm the seasons passed one by one;*
> *from morning to evening the householder makes a living,*
> *deluded and disoriented the hair turned white;*
> *right and wrong, what day will it all end?*
> *Worried and perplexed, when can it cease?*
> *Clearly and obviously there is a path to cultivate;*
> *no matter what, regardless, people are unwilling to practice.*

Dilemmas and setbacks are the creations of individuals confused by their attachments to thoughts. This sense of "I"—of individual existence—is none other than the function of grasping for thought. Emotions cannot arise externally; without the mind's participation and the chain of thoughts that follow, there is no feeling to be had.

Thoughts are created by the mind, but the ability to create

thought lies within us. It does not require external stimulations by circumstantial factors. But ordinary beings have developed a strong habitual dependence on circumstance. Due to the lack of awareness regarding his essential nature, man has become outwardly directed with a false sense of independent individuality. Ironically, this false sense of independence from the Collective causes him to be easily affected by what he perceives as his environment, particularly in terms of how he creates thoughts and feelings.

The focus on external conditions produces an unconscious manner of thinking that lacks freedom. For example, good feelings naturally arise when we are enjoying good food or receiving a compliment, but under the opposite circumstances, inevitably, we feel distress. An ordinary being's mind is easily affected by people, objects and situations that are external. Satisfaction that arises from the meeting of a grasping mind and its desired object can only be illusory. The attempt to satisfy "I,"—that mistakenly conceived notion—with thoughts that are inherently transitory perpetuates man's illusion. This attempt to find fulfillment based on illusion is the reason that so many of us find ourselves repeating the same problems or having the same negative feelings, time and time again.

The repetition of human problems is caused by attachment. Attachment is like an inner compass that directs us to a fixed point of reference from which we live our lives. The interplay between attachment and phenomena is like a pond without an outlet, circulating the stagnant water of decay, yet never finding a fresh source. The habitual flow between our attachments and the situations in our life creates deep ruts in which our life flows, and suffering is the result.

Attachment drives our conscious and subconscious behaviors, our obsessions and emotional responses to people, objects and situations. Significant examples of attachment include addiction to cigarettes or food, as well as uncontrollable rage and jealousy. In Zen, only those who have intimate knowledge with the Pure Mind—in other words, those who have eradicated the attachment to "I"—can manifest the universal truth of selflessness.

Even aspects of life that people generally perceive as consciousness or sub-consciousness are not outside the bounds of self-attachment. They still occur within the realm of ignorance between birth and death. Whether it is manifested through an individual, a social group, a cultural tradition, an ethnicity or a religion, any form of attachment to the false concept of "I" drowns out the universal truth. If we are unable to release the attachment to "I," our thoughts and decisions will be flawed—no matter how clear or conscious they might appear. To live life through self-attachment is to walk in a thick fog, enveloped by confusion.

Before enlightenment, all modes of mind functioning are centered around the false core of "I," and they operate based on the belief—the attachment—that suggests our habits define us. Nations and ethnic groups get their cultural self-perception from the aggregated habitual tendencies of the groups' members. The mind operates the way it usually does, and the habitual behaviors created by the mind are then taken as the self: "I," or "my country, my culture and my religion." These habitual beliefs and the thoughts and actions they cause prevent the essence of the original Mind to be understood. When universal truth is obscured, we find ourselves in the predicament of dualistic bondage and conflict: In the self-made bondage of attachment and the confrontations and arguments with others that are triggered by these old familiar thoughts, we lose our freedom.

Any situation may contain a brief period in which the various attachments and dependencies of the individuals or the groups are kept calm by a relative balance of external conditions. When this momentary peace happens, for a while, everyone involved will find the situation acceptable. But, inevitably feelings will change, and the attachments of someone involved will redirect his attention in a way that clouds the real problem and draws attention away from it.

Our modern culture's obsession with entertainment, television, food, drugs, cigarettes, gambling, sports, sleep, shopping and sex offer quite a selection of distractions we can use to cover up and avoid dealing with our real problems. In the same way that the individual uses these distractions, a social group can use its cultural traditions, customs, festivities, folklore and religious ideas to keep itself preoccupied.

If we focus on these distractions, we can temporarily hide the real problems, but we will not be able to resolve them, either as an individual or a group. The real solution must start from the root of the problem, the individual or the group's attachments and habitual tendencies. These beliefs and behaviors that lie deep at the core not only limit the potential of an individual or a group, but they also establish the only course in which that individual or group will develop.

All is mind-made. The karma in the mind of an individual will stay with the individual, and the shared karma of the collective group will follow the group until the individual's mind functioning or the group's collective consciousness is transformed. The ways we choose to see, the values by which we judge and the beliefs we hold create a firm cast that shapes our consciousness, both as individuals and with the collective consciousness and traditional customs of a group.

Attachment creates rigidity and patterns of repetition. Because the behaviors of each individual and group are unique and distinct from one another, friction cannot be avoided. No two people or groups are completely compatible, so in every relationship there will be a mixture of positive and negative aspects.

Compatibility brings the feeling of unity, but that compatibility is only partial. So even within the unity there is still discord. Incompatibility breeds discord, but that disagreement is not complete. Even when we disagree, there is still some measure of unity.

In the tide of rising and falling conditions, unifying and separating karmic forces become intermingled. Individuals and groups want to force every instance of a situation to unfold according to a rigid pattern of thinking, but such an attempt is impractical. It does little more than magnify the perceived gap between the expectation and the reality.

From the perspective of Zen, unenlightened beings create and trap themselves in a self-made world of illusions and expectations; they live a life of dreams within dreams. Having the best medicine is nothing compared to having a healthy body in the first place, but having the best explanation or answer to our questions cannot replace the need for introspective awareness. A true practitioner recognizes each problem and reflects inwardly to break down the inner illusion and reveal the light behind the cloud.

In the koan of the encounter of Bodhidharma, the first patriarch of Zen in China, and the second patriarch Hue-Ke, we can recognize that the circumstances of the encounter, the inward inquiry and illumination, and the destruction of attachment present the opportunity for the I-consciousness to be dissolved.

The monk Sheng-Guon stood for the whole night in deep snow that rose past his knees, seeking knowledge from Bodhidharma. "Why are you standing here?" asked Bodhidharma. "May the venerable show me compassion and open the gate of elixir that liberates all beings." Bodhidharma said to him, "The ancient Buddhas, in seeking the true dharma, were able to practice what is difficult to practice and tolerate what is difficult to tolerate. How can anyone attain the Way through inferior merit and wisdom, pride and a lack of respect for diligent effort?" Upon hearing this, Sheng-Guon cut off his left arm with a sharp knife as a demonstration of his resolve. Bodhidharma then said, "All Buddhas aspire toward the dharma with disregard for the body. Losing the arm today in front of me, it seems some genuine aspiration is still left in you."

Thus Bodhidharma took him as a student with the name Hue-Ke, who then requested of his teacher, "Please, now teach me the true dharma seal of the Buddhas." Bodhidharma knew that Hue-Ke had tried to solve his problem by seeking the answer outside himself, but since the question was really his, how could anyone answer for him?

To help Hue-Ke destroy his delusion and attachment to the outwardly directed mind, Bodhidharma said to him, "The true dharma seal of the Buddhas cannot be obtained from others." This response contradicted Hue-Ke's idea that true peace of mind could be found outside himself. Having the external outlets cut off by Bodhidharma, Hue-Ke ceased all grasping and instead turned toward himself for answers, saying, "My mind has not yet found peace. May Master help put it at ease!" At this point, Hue-Ke finally came to face his real question. Bodhidharma then said to him, "Hand me your mind, and then I shall put it at ease for you."

With this, Hue-Ke was given an opportunity to look deeply into himself; to illuminate inwardly so as to dispel his ignorance and realize that the Mind, a formless awareness that is without clinging, is originally at peace. Only by shining the light of awareness on our ignorance can the veil of the self-centered conceit of "I" be lifted in order to reveal the nature of the Mind as the universal truth. Having looked deeply within himself, Hue-Ke responded, "The mind is not to be found." Bodhidharma then replied, "Thus I have put your mind at ease."

The real problem in life is the delusion of an independent I-consciousness. This corrupted view of individual independence cannot help but produce an egoistic self-perception and interaction with others. When this self-centeredness and the karma it generates are recognized, it can then be broken down through the practice of meditation. If the awakening of an individual can trigger a collective self-reflection for a group, there is a chance to transform that group's shared karma.

Students often approach me with questions, and after listening to them for a while I ask, "What is the problem?" Some may say, for example, that they have bad karma. Clearly things have not gone well for them. However, blaming negative experiences on bad karma is often just a convenient way to avoid looking at the real issue; it is not due to recognition of the actual issue. Assigning all our problems to the karma is simply to engage another form of the mind's outward-seeking tendency. It is clear to me, whenever I hear such questions, that these students have not truly confronted their problems, they are hiding them behind the idea of "karma."

This kind of understanding is similar to applying a beautiful coat of paint over a dirty wall: The problem not only remains but will also get worse. To say there is bad karma is only half the story, since there is still a lack of clarity. Most people pick up concepts and terminologies and attempt to label what happens in their lives without clearly seeing the reality. This is the biggest problem of all. Whether in spiritual or worldly matters, as an individual or a group, the most important spiritual lesson is to really face oneself.

Spiritual seekers often over-emphasize the principle of emptiness while ignoring reality. For example, a student once told me, "The mind is all-pervasive; it manifests all of life's problems." When I asked him to clarify his real question, he said, "Reciting the sutra cannot solve my real problems, because all problems come from the mind." To this I would now respond, "The greatest problem you have is the failure to recognize your real problem. You are comparing your experiences with certain intellectual ideas or concepts in the scriptures, and you hypothesize what your question should be by using the terminologies you have learned. But if you truly want to be helped, you will need to express your real problem instead of living with a hypothetical one. This is one of the greatest delusions people have."

Many practitioners make such mistakes. Therefore, I often ask people, "What is your real question?" When facing this question, one must describe what is factual and concrete instead of giving a treatise on the terminologies of philosophical abstraction. Until we truly understand the profound meaning behind the spiritual concepts, we are simply turning our backs on the truth if we attempt to use these concepts to package a problem. Ask a false question and you will get a false answer; a question that fails to touch the root of the issues will never lead to resolution.

Life's problems are created by the mind's tendency to grasp at phenomena. Another layer of confusion is created on top of this phenomena-grasping mind when we misuse labels and terminologies. Those who see clearly, such as the Zen masters, know this tendency of ordinary beings. They avoid the trapping of labels by asking their students to describe the real meaning behind the words they use, thereby cutting through to the heart of the matter and revealing the true nature of the mind.

The term "karma," for example, refers to aspects of life, such as our physical appearance, social status, living environment, relationships with people and situations, and what we can see and hear, as well as the limitless expanse of existences in the universe. Karma results from the mind's functioning. To put it another way, the "I" in the present moment and everything in the sphere of all the existences that are connected to this "I" in the present moment are one's karma. Buddha and bodhisattva have their own karma, and each individual and group has its own unique karma as well.

But many people use the term "karma" loosely, as a substitute for describing and comprehending all unpleasant situations. They rationalize away the truth of the unpleasantness by making statements such as, "His failure was due to karma" or "Because of karma, he was killed in a car accident."

It is indeed true that karma can be used to describe all aspects of existence, but it is important to know its precise meaning and in which context it can be used productively. When we discuss spiritual practice and methods for dissolving and transforming karma, the use of the term "karma" is appropriate. It is most suitable to use the term "karma" when we focus on ways to eliminate the negative karma of ignorance and find a way past the obstacles facing an individual or a group in order to create a positive karma—both in the spiritual realm and in the mundane.

A label is just a label, so it is not your real problem; only your real problem matters. It is ignorant to use a label as a substitute for the real problem, since it only clouds the real issue.

## Let Go of Labels, No More Excuses

When a belief we hold—either as an individual or as a group—is challenged, we usually attempt to validate our point through defensive arguments and to convince those who hold different opinions. These responses lead to confrontational interactions. Defensiveness only perpetuates an individual's original attachment, like adding frost over snow, which complicates and worsens the situation.

Unfortunately, many people take pride in the ability to defend or "stand up" for their attachments, not realizing they are deepening the hole for their downfall. Defending our attachments only strengthens them. This is why a Zen master would never approve of the opinions produced by a deluded mind, nor would he provide intellectual answers to a student's questions.

Instead, the Zen teacher tries to cut off a practitioner's mental tendency of grasping ideas or conceptual answers outside himself. By cutting off paths to the outside, he creates opportunities for inner reflection and inquiry into his beliefs about the source and truth of his problem. Once the answers produced by the outwardly grasping mind are surrendered and old concepts are dropped for good, the real answer will emerge from the mind.

This is the unique teaching style of the Zen masters. People who do not understand this may judge Zen teachers as being somewhat unreasonable, but in truth they possess the most profound compassion for their students. They demonstrate real compassion by refusing to give prepackaged answers, lead students down the wrong path or add to the students' attachments. Instead, they cut off the habitual tendency through stern admonitions that lead the students to the door of realization. A writing on the entrance to the retreat quarters of a Zen master said it all:

*No trespassing,*
*This place cannot be known to man;*
*No recognition of appearances,*
*Do not complain for the lack of courtesy.*
*Here is the Joyful Dwelling of the True Self.*

The dwelling of Zen masters is not like anything you will encounter in the everyday world, and you cannot understand it in the same way

Another obstacle to change, besides our defensiveness, is the inability to put our understanding into action. It is common to say, "I'm just not disciplined enough to dedicate myself to practice" as an excuse for the lack of commitment. Because ignorance tends to overshadow our intelligence, we rationalize our inability to change by seeking sympathy from others, assigning faults to others or claiming a lack of time and place. But placing blame outside of ourselves is just self-deception, and in it there is no chance of attaining real progress.

Many practitioners cannot benefit from the teachings and even cause others to slander Buddhism. Although they may know the concepts intellectually, they lack the willingness to work toward the actual practice of self-reflection. "Like painting empty waves without any fish or a beautifully embroidered flower that has no fragrance," these spiritual seekers are eager to try to convert to the great benefits of their beliefs, but it is clear that they have not changed themselves for the better.

When people do lip service to Buddhism without doing the work, they render Buddhism ineffective and give it a bad name. Practicing spirituality with our old habitual tendencies is futile; it only adds another layer of spiritual attachment and it is an abuse of the Buddha dharma. No rationalization or intellectual concept can save us or resolve any of our problems. Instead, it will cause the stagnation of both dharma and the problem. Treating Buddhism as an intellectual exercise is not a true path of practice but merely a means by which the problem is exacerbated. Unfortunately, many of today's practitioners make this error.

Using spiritual teachings as the tools and means for transforming the self-attachment and habitual tendencies accumulated since time immemorial is the only path toward the achievement of transformation. Hunger cannot be satiated by drawing a piece of cake on paper. There is an ancient Zen saying that goes like this:

*Bodhidharma brought not a single word from the West,*
*Nothing other than practicing with this very Mind,*
*If you wish to indulge in theoretical discussion,*
*The tip of the fountain pen shall dry up the Dong-Ting Lake.*

The truth is not easy to find. Only diligent, energetic effort can break through the ignorance and unveil the manifestation of the truth, the Pure Mind. The truth is the universal principle, not an explanation of mundane ideas. If your practice cannot become intimate with the universal principle, you will continue in ignorance.

Spiritual practice is about self-transformation. It is about transforming the dilemma created by the false sense of an independent "I" and the lack of inner-strength resulting from a narrow-minded perspective of reality. The Buddha taught numerous methods of spiritual cultivation to different individuals, but the ordinary person holds onto his attachment and is therefore unable to realize his own true nature. While spiritual practice requires inner-strength and wisdom, many practitioners have misunderstood this concept and therefore believe they lack the qualities needed to engage in spiritual practice. But speculating on whether or not you have sufficient merit to practice is not productive. The more practical question to ask is how you can find a way to resolve the problems that already exist in your life.

Sometimes we know that change is necessary but are unable to achieve it, or we recognize the problem but are unwilling to accept reality. In either case, there is no alternative but to remain trapped between these two difficult positions. Eventually, frustration leads to depression and exhaustion, and finally we completely resign from the attempt to improve our situation.

When we reach this state of resignation to the situation, our life stagnates in futility. It is like attempting to light a lamp without any fuel; it's just a waste of the wick.

Unless we are willing to work in the present moment, there is no chance of resolving any of the present difficulties, and no chance of accumulating merit and wisdom. Without taking action now, there is no possibility of increasing merit and obtaining the opportunity to change our karma in the future. Life will remain stuck in the present reality, and we cannot be freed to find the possibility of a better future.

There is no end to the excuses we can make. But the reality is that we all live with the limitations imposed by our attachments and the burden of our ignorance. We should not resign ourselves and hide behind delusions; we must resolve to break through our mistaken understanding. We can achieve this breakthrough by seeing through the delusions we have about the independent self and overcoming the obstacles on the path that have been created by dualism—the gap between the individual and the Collective.

Comparing practitioners in terms of spiritual progress serves no useful purpose. By nature, comparison is a dualistic mental activity that solidifies the false sense of "I." Some people present themselves as possessing lesser capacity or aptitude, but they still try to criticize others as impractical, claiming they are taking the wrong path or a long path. This attitude is certainly the manifestation of a superiority complex driven by inner pride.

In spiritual practice, nothing is more precious than having the right view of the universal truth. The distance between our present self and the complete actualization of the Way depends on our degree of ignorance and attachment. Every house has its own view of the bright moon. The pace of our spiritual attainment has nothing to do with others.

Buddhism is a path of inner cultivation, but because attachment is created by us it is up to us to eradicate it. This idea is clear and easily understood by all. Spiritual capacity, or "aptitude," is not a "given" attribute; it is the result of our previous efforts. Whether mundane or spiritual, all distinctions between good and bad or right and wrong come from the correct or incorrect way we apply ourselves. Because we have made choices in the past, the circumstances in which we find ourselves in the present are the result of our own effort. In that sense, we are solely responsible for ourselves. It is important to refrain from making comparisons with others.

I have often heard people say things such as, "He has more time for practice because he is rich and does not need to work," or "She has more flexibility with time because she is still unmarried, but I have responsibilities for my husband and children." The truth, however, is that even for those who supposedly have time, some will choose to practice but others will prefer to stay home and watch television, go shopping or spend the day sleeping. They will drift through life, lamenting the seeming purposelessness of their present and future existence as they drown in the ocean of vexation, lamenting their lack of accomplishment until the very end.

Countless people have failed to recognize the fundamental wrongness of independent existence and, because they don't understand, they have squandered opportunities for spiritual practice. First, they are burdened by the challenging circumstances of life, and secondly they lack the proper guidance to change their circumstances. These problems accumulate over time and heavily burden the future. This is the truth of life for humankind.

My students in Zen training will sometimes proudly report that they are diligent in practice, but I often counter with the view that, while it is encouraging to hear of their efforts, there is still a strong I-consciousness beneath what they are saying. So, they should continue their training with even more effort. The true meaning of diligence is the continuous practice of letting go of the habitually self-centered tendency to grasp at external phenomena.

The moment the I-consciousness latches onto any situation, it signifies the unconscious attempt to separate from the Collective. The Zen analogy for this is to cut away a blister from perfectly good flesh. The truly diligent spiritual practitioner is the one who can transform the I-consciousness in ideas and life's troubling situations, and use the transformed understanding to directly experience and manifest the universal truth.

## The Light Within All

We must be proactive in making the right preparation for change. First, we must recognize the problems confronting us and hold the deep conviction that those problems are our own creation. Our vexations cannot arise from Buddhism, since they existed long before any of us came in contact with the teaching. Neither do vexations come from other people because, in the absence of others, we are still beset by issues that must be resolved. All problems come from a mind that is out of control, and personal vexations can only come from the person experiencing them. Since the human mind is the origin of our vexations, we must first lift the veil of intellectual theories and doctrines that obstructs our awareness. Only then can we can begin to see the nature of our problems.

Only a fervent desire to solve a problem can spur the motivation for awakening, and this fervent desire is the beginning of a path toward resolution. Without this desire, any discussion of the problem will fail to resolve it and might even end up obscuring or marginalizing the real problem. As when you visit a physician, if you cannot describe the symptoms, how can the doctor offer any help? Healing requires the recognition of the need for help, the ability to describe the symptoms and cooperate in the treatment process and follow with regular checkups. The path to healing consists of acknowledging the signs of illness, and preparing to face and go through the process of treatment.

The awakening of an individual provides an opportunity for the destruction of his or her participation in the shared ignorance. The Buddha, through a profound recognition of the suffering that aroused the desire for freedom, taught his disciples to reflect inwardly and awaken to the true nature of the Mind. This awakening is what leads to the state of sainthood, to being among those who are able to actualize the universal truth in their lives.

Spiritual practitioners should know that the source of phenomena is the Mind. The Mind comprises the indivisibility of the individual and the Collective. When the individual replaces the false I-consciousness with the Mind's innate capacity to dissolve attachments, merges with the original state and integrates with the Collective, the universal truth becomes manifest. This is the process for solving any problem at its source.

You should practice confronting your own issues in order to resist domination by the false I-consciousness and achieve mastery over your mind by breaking through inner delusions. Buddha taught his students to see the true causes of any problem and apply various skillful means directly to those causes. We must squarely and truly face our predicaments in order to move our lives in the direction we desire. But today we unconsciously tend to focus our attention externally as we try to solve our problems.

This tendency to focus externally is the greatest of all problems, because we should look inwardly in order to see our own karma instead of looking outwardly upon the karma of others. Without an awareness of our own karmic seeds, karmic consciousness and karmic results, how can we possibly have any clarity about another person's karma?

A particular Zen saying goes like this: *"Even one who is deaf can sing an exotic song. Pleasant or out of pitch, he does not know."* How can a person who does not know his own mind actually understand the meaning of Buddha's teaching? How can he have knowledge regarding the karma and disposition of various sentient beings? Many of Buddha's disciples are enlightened because they have the willingness and ability to see any problem clearly and will make efforts that pacify the agitated mind according to the Buddha's instruction. They have prepared for spiritual tasks—the process of recognizing suffering and its cause, making the effort to transform one's painful karma and become liberated from the prison of a false, independent I-consciousness—by fostering the energy for diligence with a sincere wish to be freed from the suffering of such karma. This is the clear, direct path for the transformation of sentient beings toward the state of freedom, the true prescription for the alleviation of worldly woes.

Invariably, the delusion of I-consciousness comes with suffering. It is inherently unstable and groundless, and it lacks awareness. All forms of suffering come from this obscured state of mind, which in Buddhism is called "self-attachment." A Zen master once said: *"All beings possess the great luminosity, but one only finds darkness when looking for it."* This describes the plight of an unenlightened individual. The Mind is the source of all phenomena. Without inner peace, suffering is unavoidable—regardless of any effort. When there is no peace of mind, it is easy to believe our problem is created by others, but how can that be so? If problems are caused externally—in the belief that they belong to others—then why do we suffer?

The suffering we feel does not come from external sources, for if that were the case there would be a connection with us. This is a very important concept to remember: Any form of spiritual or emotional suffering must have its root within us.

Actually, it is not necessary to speculate about the cause of suffering. It is obvious that suffering is a state of mind in which there is no peace; it is out of control. As long as the I-consciousness remains with us, there will not be peace; only the eradication of this I-consciousness can resolve our problems.

The I-consciousness is essentially the creation of the mind, which was originally pure. Because all phenomena lack any substantial existence, it is futile to seek stability in phenomena with a deluded I-consciousness. It is completely unnecessary, and such stability is impossible to attain. In a similar manner, any attempt to stabilize a culture built on the false foundation of collective delusion will only create problems that cannot be resolved. To engage such an attempt is to take up an impossible mission for human culture and history. Since ancient times, this deluded approach has been the greatest frustration and lamentation for humanity.

Modern people are poorly prepared to face their individual issues, let alone the greater problem that stands before all humanity. The delusory existence of the individual causes a rising anxiety that seeks relief with drugs and physical appearance, money, fraudulence, conceptual abstraction, and various forms of mental and physical laziness—all of these serve only to divert the individual's attention from the fundamental cause of anxiety. If we cover a beehive with a thin coat of paint, the threat of a breakout is still imminent.

The emphasis on knowledge that is based on materialism, such as medicine, biology, economics and technology, can only provide occasional, unrelated clues from the vast complex of multifaceted dynamics in the realm of phenomena. Such knowledge is applied in order for man to formulate theories on how reality operates. Even though these theories are rigid and restrictive in their depth and breadth of understanding, they have been tried and applied to society at large for the sake of bringing stability and prosperity to human life.

But the flaw of this logical, analytical framework is clear: Just as it is impossible to fathom the depth of the ocean by measuring it with a dipper the size of a seashell, or to perceive the heavens through a slender bamboo pipe, there is an unimaginably large gap between the actual truth and what can be grasped. With regard to human faith, similar situations arise when people attempt to use that which is inflexible to understand that which is formless and impermanent. This approach shows an ignorance of the fact that the truth is beyond any form. Any attempt to communicate that which is beyond form with that which is of form is ultimately limited and unsatisfactory.

The ancient Lin-Ji school of Zen was founded by a famed master of the same name. During his life, many students came to him in the quest for understanding. Whenever the master found a disciple who was burdened by undigested concepts regarding truth, he would say, "*There is a formless true being, illuminating wondrous lights at your six doors of sense faculties; do you recognize him?*" Or he would say, "*Pay *attention to each footstep, and maintain your practice with mindfulness."* He knew that once a disciple had accumulated many undigested, half-baked conceptual ideas about the truth, his mind functioning would be guided by such mental rubbish and would thus derive no benefit from any new idea. It would be similar to adding another heavy iron chain to his neck, already burdened by the many iron chains he had previously acquired. It would serve no purpose other than to provide another topic of conversation.

Based on his profound wisdom, Lin-Ji recognized the defect in the activities of the I-consciousness and the student's tendency to perceive true realization as the acquisition of knowledge and ideas, and he recognized that the attainment of these theories has the potential to exacerbate the attachment to false views of reality. It is very difficult for such a student to set aside his views in order to adopt new ways of seeing reality; it is difficult for such a student to attain enlightenment because he or she has mistaken the deluded self as true and substantial in existence and his mind has become bound by the habitual tendencies that the deluded self has created.

Man, in every moment, gives rise to thoughts and then identifies those thoughts as his own. Thus we believe in our own interpretation of reality and what we hear and see. We believe strongly in ourselves, and we behave as though we have attained the infallibility of sainthood. But this is a serious error. Zen provides the training process so that we, with our otherwise narrow and rigid mind, can transform and transcend the limitations of habitually self-centered perception and judgment.

Just as man has dug his own grave through his flawed definition of reality, which has molded a false sense of independent selfhood, the same process can be applied in order to de-construct the false self, shovel by shovel. Thought by thought, we can build a path out of the grave of deep attachment by filling it with right thoughts, bridging the false gap between the individual and the Collective.

Even though we talk about the gap between the truth and that which is delusory, at the moment of awakening we realize it is nothing but a dream. *"An old house and an abandoned land they are; there is no rest from cultivation until the harvest."* To arrive at this place, we must be diligent in our practice and effort; eventually we will walk out of the deep, dark abyss of ignorance, back into the sunshine, where the mind can manifest its original clarity and luminosity and be completely at ease anywhere. This is the ultimate goal of Zen.

We should not let our living conditions or our age dictate whether or not we can consider making changes. We must seize every opportunity to practice. Time does not wait. The ancients said: *"Let us not wait until old age to seek the Way, for the lone graves are all those who died young."* How can a sense of urgency not be aroused in any man of intelligence who hears such a statement?

As we ask whether we have properly prepared for practice, we should reflect inwardly in earnest. If we find that we have prepared, then true change will naturally occur, with the perfect timing. When we recognize the reality we have created, as well as its causes and results, we face it with acceptance and the willingness to make change with the right thoughts. We must persevere in our practice, one good thought at a time, as we open new doors toward the future.

Contemplating these thoughts, you stand at the threshold of the doorway of Zen. You are about to begin the process of dissolving the false self as you walk toward the freeing reality of the universal truth.

The Light of Innate Nature, rarely recognized in life,

Pervades all the corners of the Ocean

and the edges of Heaven;

It has fallen to the fetters of scattered phenomena,

Have compassion for the unconsciously imprisoned.

# 3 MANIFEST THROUGH KARMA, LIVE WITH KARMA

Dong-Po's poem went eastward of the river,

Li Bai drank to the spirit in the Moon;

Kicking over Men in front of the Huang-He Pagoda,

Foot ache has remained to this very day.

Many people ask, "How can I find the spiritual book or teacher that is right for me?" This question is actually quite a contradiction. Every individual has his own prejudice and belief, so he has no choice but to use them in deciding what is correct and appropriate. If the books I recommend do not fit the preference of individual's pre-programming, he will most likely reject them. Even if he does manage to accept my recommendation, his inner attachment will probably resist, causing him to find the concepts described by the recommended books unacceptable or questionable. Consequently, he will set them aside.

The type of spiritual guidance we encounter and accept is generally determined by the ideas that are already present in our mind. The manifestation of karma is based on the false I-consciousness—meaning the structural and functional pattern of mental habits—and the mental state created by the particular tendencies of the I-consciousness will respond to books and teachings that resonate with our karma.

For example, before learning about Zen you may have more

interest in other spiritual or philosophical teachings. This is because your individual karmic stream has not yet connected with Zen. An individual's I-consciousness triggers different karma and therefore different kinds of spiritual guidance from moment to moment; an individual actually has neither freedom of choice nor clarity regarding all the factors present within a situation. Since an ordinary being establishes the false I-consciousness as his true self, even the idea of freedom of choice in what we perceive and how we value it is nothing but a delusion of the I-consciousness.

## Carefully Choose the Right View

When attempting to cultivate a spiritual view or understanding, it is important to be cautious. Because the unenlightened individual is not yet able to discern either reality or what would be beneficial, once a false view or understanding enters the mind, it will be too late to realize it. Our digestive system will warn us about contaminated food through physical pain and discomfort, but there is no such safety mechanism for spiritual practice. Once a false view is established through the reading of certain books or following certain spiritual teachers, students may be led toward an incorrect course of practice. A false view combined with its incorrect practice can quickly affect an individual's belief system and behavior pattern, directly impacting daily life. That false view becomes firmly rooted in the mind and serves as the governing principle of the misguided practitioner's life.

It would be very difficult to change that belief or perspective later. Like a computer programmed to operate in certain ways, a belief or a spiritual view, once firmly established, manifests reality in a manner that tends to reinforce the belief or view. This reinforcement prevents the individual from recognizing and extricating himself from the flawed circuitries in the web of his belief system and the suffering he will inevitably experience. The formation of any false view is a serious matter, because its impact can extend across the infinite horizon of the future.

As part of our mental fabric, each of us who is not enlightened has certain false views upon which we naturally depend in order to live our lives, not knowing there is an alternative. The interaction between those false views and the environment forms a negative cycle. It is much like washing a dirt brick in the mud: The more it is washed, the dirtier it becomes.

Our attachment to false views is like the skin attached to the flesh, since it is literally a part of who we are. To separate the skin from the flesh, we must use a knife. Similarly, separating false views from the mind takes a great deal of training and effort so that the mental agitation the false views create can be pacified, allowing us the chance for inner reflection that—once it is strong enough—can destroy the false I-consciousness.

The right view and the right guidance will manifest when a disciple has a pure, sincere motivation to attain the Way. The mind is formless, like the Great Void. To engage in spiritual practice is to build a bridge and use it to traverse a vast emptiness. It is a serious undertaking, since much time could be wasted by placing one wrong step in this vast emptiness. All spiritual seekers should tread lightly and carefully, making each step with a pure, sincere intention and humility for learning.

We carry the views we have acquired with us on our journey, and they cause each moment of our present and future life. When we use false views from the past, we create—from moment to moment—life after life of unconscious mind functioning. The process continues, causing an infinite accumulation of karma with serious consequences. I often remind people that the karmic consequence of propagating false views is more serious than killing, because once a false view is established it is extremely difficult to remove.

There is a precautionary saying that goes, "A view entering the mind is like mixing oil in the batter, impossible to retrieve." Every spiritual practitioner should heed this warning. It is so difficult to change the way you think, because your beliefs have wrapped themselves so tightly around your mind that they have literally become the basis of how you behave and live your life. Take right now, for example. As you read my words, you are going through a certain thought pattern. On a certain level, the fixed pattern in your mind is guiding you to selectively pick up particular ideas, ideas which resonate with your beliefs. These are the concepts that "make sense" to you, based on the conclusion reached through your habitual pattern of thought.

If I were to tell you that all your ideas have been false, what would your reaction be? You might feel a sense of inner conflict; you might feel depressed or try to argue otherwise. In situations where a person's habitual tendency or thought pattern cannot find its accustomed outlet or object of grasping, he becomes lost, like a spaceship drifting in the void with neither the power of propulsion nor any real direction. At such a moment, the individual will either change course in order to adopt new ideas or will try to rationalize and validate his habits, making them stronger and even more impenetrable so that he can continue in his old ways.

Even the idea of changing yourself can be a subtle form of self-deception because, after all, such an idea has come from a mind with attachments and habitual tendencies. This attempt at new thinking and new action could simply be the same attachment with different packaging. When you neither desire nor recognize the need to change, your life will remain the same. But for people who are always on a quest for change, genuine change does not necessarily occur; their habitual pattern is the desire for change, not the desire for a genuine opportunity for transformation. If your desire to change cannot escape the grip of your habitual tendency, your effort will not yield results. Real change demands appropriate methods.

All thoughts are created from the selfless purity of the mind. But the deluded individual has become attached to the thought that has arisen from the mind, and he has conceived the idea of an independent "self" in order to have the ability to create thoughts. He gives rise to thoughts from the originally pure mind through the conceived self. This close connection between the individual's delusion and the thought pattern of the self is what we call self-attachment.

More specifically, mind functioning is controlled by unconscious habits. These habits are the result of experiences accumulated when the false interacted with the environment. Each individual's self has unique ideas that are mutually exclusive, so there the potential for contradiction always exists. The individual unconsciously believes in his own ideas, so even objectivity is not outside the realm of habit and personality traits.

The thought that is manifested each moment from an individual's mind is the only possible thought that can be had at that moment. However, being the only thought does not make the thought right; it is simply the inevitability of having no alternative. These unavoidable perceptions and judgments create the "have-to" in life: right because it has to, wrong because it has to, contradictory because it has to, and must since it has to. These have-to elements are the key problems in life.

Do you believe you can find the right knowledge, teachers and guidance for your life? It is a universal truth that each of us has the ability to believe we are right. But we need to ponder more deeply when we consider if the object of our belief is correct. To believe in what you believe is irrelevant to the question of whether you can find the right teaching or a good teacher. Most people are unable to achieve contact with the universal truth because doing so requires the purest, most sincere aspiration. It takes a strong determination and willingness to sacrifice yourself for the sake of the Way.

Many spiritual practices are focused on stress relief and planting seeds for a positive future. This approach dilutes the core of the teaching by molding itself for the popular culture—it broadens the appeal of the teaching, but it changes the original meaning of the message. There is a saying: "First motivate through desire, then guide them to the Buddha's wisdom." Modern-day Buddhism has many skillful means to introduce the teaching to the public. While it is important to arouse faith and interest, it is more important to guide beings into the liberating wisdom. If it does not put people on the path to enlightenment, Buddhism is no different from any other spiritual teaching.

When we find ourselves stuck, unable to progress spiritually, it can be because we do not have the right view, determination and a clear goal. Or it can be because the teaching on which we rely, though apparently sensible, actually contradicts the universal principle. It is not simply a matter of doing seated meditation, chanting and reciting Buddha's name or mantra. Spiritual practice is about having the ability to create a joyful, fulfilling life and eventually obtain complete liberation from our limitations and suffering. If we cannot accomplish this, how can we convince others?

Man lives under the self-deception that further efforts through his old karmic pattern can produce a happy life. It is a great delusion to credit any particular way of life as being the source of happiness. When a person entertains this idea, it shows that he has not yet recognized the reality; he lives within his self-created trap. Wisdom and merit are the qualities that truly matter in life, as they allow the individual to choose the right path for his life. Therefore, the key to a good life is the cultivation of wisdom and merit.

Using an appropriate method to eliminate habitual tendencies will bring forth mindful awareness. This awareness is wisdom; it is the view of a pure mind, vast without boundary. When we can compose our thoughts, attachments and greed are eliminated, and merits are generated. We must see that wisdom is the root of all existence in the mind, and that in the presence of this wisdom the individual and the Collective merge as one without distinction. The ability to handle situations with wisdom in order to live the life of Pure Mind is a merit. Lacking merit and wisdom, we remain in the darkness of dualistic ignorance, and our minds function with delusion, causing an endless wheel of karmic consequences.

### Understand Causality to Take Charge of Our Fate

What is the true meaning of causality? When we continuously push forward in a fixed direction with unconscious mind functioning, we build up a habitual pattern around a false sense of self. Like a seed, in the presence of proper conditions, it grows into a great tree that bears fruit, which spreads their seeds farther and wider.

Our present circumstances and personal endowments are already the result of karma, like the ripened fruits on the tree. Man has always sought to change the fruit directly into something else, but it is impossible to do so. To harvest different fruit, we must start from the cause—the source—and plant the right seeds. Ironically, the human tendency is to want different fruit but to be so trapped in our old ways that the effort of planting new seeds is too great.

The present reality of our life is the concrete display of the principle of causality. The right seed might appear to be small, but it is actually the only guarantee that the desired result will be obtained. Having thousands of kinds of mistaken fruits cannot compare, in any measurable way, to the benefit of having the right seed.

Because man has over a long time cultivated the incorrect results from his habits, change can only be achieved by reversing the forces and direction of these habitual tendencies. This must start by arousing mindful awareness. It has been said: "Do not disregard small good, do not permit small evil." Refraining from acting in negative ways, in even the smallest things, opens up opportunities for positive transformations. Mindful awareness is critical to making this type of change. Slowly make the right effort to change and cultivate the necessary factors, and eventually the wonderful fruit of your mindful effort will ripen.

A new life comes from a new way of thinking; from a new set of thoughts and ideas that replace the unconscious mode of mind functioning. The emergence of new ideas marks the beginning of the destruction of the old pattern. Only by destroying your attachments can you open the doors to a new way of life. Letting go of your unconscious mode of thinking allows your mind to openly pick up new concepts and release the faults of the old ways. In terms of practice, you should redirect your awareness inwardly to halt the stream of wandering thoughts and rein in the tendency to grasp at phenomena. This redirection will help you stop pursuing outer phenomena.

Having thoughts that are related to what is happening around you only leads you farther down the stream of delusion. False I-consciousness begins when we attempt to grasp phenomena. Once we are under the domination of the I-consciousness, we have no choice but to drift along with the karmic unfolding of fantasies and imaginations, lost in the endless cycle of change.

Knowing this, we must instead train ourselves to reverse the flow of birth and death of the phenomenal realm, calming the commotion of the phenomenon-grasping mind. We must dismantle the unconscious mode of thinking and reacting that is attached to form and break through the falsehood of the I-consciousness in order to reach the pure, unborn, undestroyed Mind Ground. When we reach this place of understanding, we will have returned from the confused path of birth and death to the unborn, unchanging original awareness of the Mind.

The presence of distress and suffering should be recognized as the exertion of the I-consciousness, which tries to maintain its independent, isolated existence from the wholeness of reality. This attempt to separate the self from its environment manifests as a predicament for the individual who, being unable to find a clear path out of his predicament, inevitably experiences a fundamental restlessness within himself. Everything already present in life is like the ripened fruit on the tree; these fruits are the consequences of seeds already sown.

Because reality is here, we must learn to determine what seeds were planted to bring forth these fruits. The presence of an apple indicates that apple seeds were planted, and that the tree arising from the seed has borne fruit. Remember that because all phenomena are the products of the mind, the reality of this moment is the end result of seeds—specifically, thoughts and actions—that have been sown in the past.

We are the farmers of our own gardens, our lives. If the harvest is not what we had hoped for, then we must reflect upon our understanding in regard to the true meaning of life. Having carefully reflected on that, we can then correct our thoughts and plant the right seeds for the desired results. Change requires both time and effort; we need to nurture the new seeds diligently and patiently without planting the old seeds again due to carelessness. Today's society places a premium on speed and on shortcuts that supposedly save time, instead of emphasizing the effort needed for the desired outcome. Anyone who is unwilling to commit the energy and time for change will end up planting the wrong seeds repeatedly, and will ultimately live with the unfortunate result of his creation.

Some people see meditation practice as a kind of panacea that can miraculously make all problems disappear. Such an idea is merely a delusion. Meditation, like other practices, is not magic. Those who propagate or believe in false teachings may tell fantastic stories that are not necessarily true. Teachers of deviant arts may guarantee their followers expedient methods for the attainment of a good life, but even worse is the fact that those who are easily taken in by such promises—even to the extent of giving away all their possessions—are trying to find shortcuts to the good life. The appeal of an "effort-free" path that promises happiness is simply a reflection of an unwillingness to face inner indolence, lack of motivation and profound ignorance.

There is no way to change reality without time, effort and determination. Look carefully at any method that promises to be easy and able to deliver quick results. Delusion is the belief of fools. Regardless of how short a path is, we must still take one step at a time in order to reach the destination. A willingness to embrace the new and different opens up opportunities for change. Having the desire for a better future is a good thing, but it is foolish to ignore our present reality.

If we experience a problem, it does not come from outside. If it were truly something external, then it would be neither a part of our life experience nor a deciding factor in our life. When I meet students for the first time, I often ask, "Is anything troubling you?" Usually, the answer is yes. I will remind them that whatever they experience as challenging is not something external. Problems are the result of an agitated mind, of an inherently unstable mental condition caused by the false sense of "I."

The "I" is the result of the mind's identification with the thoughts it has created. This "I" is surrounded by an environment that is manifested from the same mind and is restless in this environment because of the perceived conflict created by the illusory separation of what is inner and what is outer. The outer environment is a creation of the mind, and it becomes a source of disturbance to the false "I."

Unless we destroy the pattern of self-attachment giving rise to the grasping of phenomena, there will be no end to the disturbances that arise from the environment. Thoughts and phenomena are subject to constant change. To hold onto a thought arising from the mind as "my thought" and grasp the results that the mind causes to occur is essentially an act of duality. It is unstable and changing by nature. This is the reason the false self is always restless. This restlessness prevents the mind from consciously giving rise to thoughts. Once we can appreciate the fact that the false self is the actual source of all vexations, we will gain a sense of certainty regarding the source of our problems.

All the various forms of spiritual practice are only skillful means for calming the mind's afflictions. They help us to detach from the habitual thoughts that have created the false I-consciousness, so that we can experience our essential oneness with the Collective and the true nature of life. To engage in any particular spiritual practice or take part in any religious ceremony does not guarantee that real change will occur. It is simply a tool for training the mind.

Only by understanding and letting go of the pattern of mind functioning in which we deludedly and unconsciously grasp our thought as "I" can we liberate ourselves from the cocoon created by the false "I," the thoughts that surround the mind. Once we are liberated, the lively and liberated Pure Mind can be manifested. Once we know that vexations and problems are the consequences of a mind that has lost touch with its original purity, we can understand how to apply these methods of practice in daily life and thereby uplift every aspect of our existence.

### Sowing the Seeds of One's Experiences

I hear some people voice certain doubts: *If the mind does stop defining and discriminating the various forms of existence, how can I know what is real? What else is left in this world?* Actually, when all delusory discrimination stops, whatever is left will be the real world, the real self, the Pure Mind and its collective manifestation. Truth will not cease to exist without our definition. In fact, truth disappears when we live by the definitions created by our habitual thinking.

In his *Fang-Tzuen Discourse*, the fourth patriarch of Zen instructed Master Fa-Rong in this way:

*Phenomena is neither attractive nor repulsive,*

*Attractiveness and repulsiveness both arise from the mind,*

*Without forcing a label on the truth,*

*From where would delusion come?*

*Free of delusion,*

*The True Mind's awareness is all-pervasive,*

*Rest at ease with the Mind as is,*

*There is no antidote to be administered,*

*Thus the ever-present Dharmakaya simply is,*

*Neither changing nor transitory.*

The body, mind and thoughts, the environment and all forms of existence manifested by the Mind penetrate and merge with each other in every moment. There is no "inside the Mind" or "outside the Mind," because the appearances of phenomena are not separated by time.

What is the cause of existence? How does the principle of causality work? The concept of causality is a profound concept in Buddhism. In a single instance of the Mind's functioning, we manifest the entirety of phenomena that includes our thoughts, our body and our environment. The essence and the function of the Mind are non-dualistic. The pure, empty Mind is the singular cause of all phenomena. The functioning of the pure, empty Mind gives rise to thoughts and creates the energy of the world we experience. Thoughts are the products of the Mind's functioning; they instantaneously appear with all related phenomena from the Collective, which is the Mind. Therefore, thought does not precede phenomena.

Some people assume that thoughts put phenomena in motion. However, this is not the ultimate truth. Thought is a product of the Mind. It appears and disappears instantaneously. Therefore, thought cannot give rise to another thought or phenomena. The true source of all things is the empty, selfless pure Mind, which gives rise to all things from its selfless, empty nature. This Mind is the first cause of all things. It is neither a nihilistic nothingness nor a materialistic existence with a tangible form. The first cause is formless and selfless, a true presence of luminosity. The ancients called it "the cause without a cause." Only those who have penetrated the true nature of the Mind can experience this cause without a cause.

Master Yung-Jia once said:

*Just when the Mind functions,*
*There is no mind to function with,*
*Without intent, the Mind simply functions,*
*Functioning just in emptiness.*

The Mind is not to be found, but its functions permeate the universe. In Zen we hear the phrase, "the sound of one hand clapping," but how can one hand make any sound? The instant the Mind functions, it verifies the function itself, and thus the phenomenon is born. Because the nature of the Mind is empty and non-dualistic, the instant it functions emptiness permeates all forms of existence that arise from it. Similarly, all forms of existence merge with the empty nature of the Mind. The function and essence of the Mind mutually permeate and penetrate, containing one another.

The Sixth Patriarch's Platform Sutra addresses the relationship of function and essence: "*At the instance of functioning, the essence is imminent in the functioning; at the instance of non-functioning, the functioning is imminent in the essence.*" The essence is empty and formless, but from this essence arise the functions and forms according to the principle of causality, or dependent origination. Among all possible functions, the grasping of thought as the self results in the establishment of a false, independent "I." This false "I," created when we grasp a small part of the essence of the Mind as our independent physical body and its attachment to thoughts, forms the basis of how we live and handle life's various situations. It becomes the structure of our reality.

Here is another way to understand the relationship between the essence and the function of the Mind: The instant any individual thinks or acts, he manifests the functioning of the Collective; in that moment, he is the manifestation of the Collective functioning. Because of this relationship, in the Collective all movement is complete and all goodness is present. When the individual ceases to function, he merges back into the empty essence of the Collective.

The functioning is the essence, and the stillness is free of any thought. The individual is the functioning of the Collective, and the Collective is the essence of the individual. This is the ultimate relationship between essence and function. In real life, man gives rise to different functions of the Mind, and each different function comes with different phenomena and thought. The great differences between life and the circumstances of different individuals can be explained by the principle of causality, as it is illustrated here.

Equality is another key spiritual concept. Equality in this context means that all beings possess the same innate ability to function with the Mind, and different Mind functioning will bring about different circumstances, perhaps pleasant or unpleasant, through the impartial operating principle of causality. In other words, the nature of the Mind is the same for all; the innate ability to function with the Mind is the same for all; the principle governing the relationships between mental functioning and its result remain the same for all; and a result, once manifested, inevitably becomes the reality of the one who has created it. The result is also the same for all. From this perspective, there is true equality among all beings.

Allow me to elaborate on this point. Every individual possesses the same innate capacity of the Mind, which can give rise to various functions. Every function creates thoughts and corresponding phenomena in life, and finally everyone makes use of the Mind and will live with the result of how he or she has used the Mind. Behind everything that happens as a result of Mind functioning, there is a reason. Because existence itself is concrete, existence ultimately embodies the principle behind the existence. If there is no principle for existence, there will be no existence.

Because there is existence there must also be a principle governing its creation. People like to complain about why things have happened to them or how things have occurred in a certain way, or they will blame God or others for being unfair. The cause within the result is the principle, and the ripening of fruit occurs based on its principle.

The equanimous mind understands that the essence of the Mind is the same for all beings. The ability to function, the principle of causality, the principle governing the dependent arising of phenomena, and the fact that the creator must live with the result of his creation are all true and equally applicable to all beings. While the appearances among all beings can be extremely variable—the rich, the poor, the healthy, the sick, the venerated, the ignored, those with social status, the working class, the farmers, the merchants and so forth—beneath all that, each individual possesses the same nature of Mind in accordance with the universal truth.

Life is like a farm: If a farmer has failed to harvest what he expected, should he even be surprised? If the result of one's labor is less than satisfactory, a certain degree of adjustment will be necessary. In order to harvest different fruits, you must plant different seeds. If you only have expectation but you have not made the required change in terms of cultivation, how can the result be any different?

The same concept is applicable to our lives. We are the owners of our habits. Once it becomes clear to us that only we can generate our thoughts, we realize it is impossible for others to take responsibility for our habits and situations. Then the logical next step is to make a change by starting with the causes. This is the only sensible and effective starting point. What happens to us, our reality, is absolutely fair and reasonable, because every manifestation of reality has a cause. It serves no purpose to complain about external circumstances. It is futile to point fingers at one another, and any negative feelings are simply the contamination and abnormality covering the natural state of the Mind, taking us farther away from the truth. Complaining only wastes valuable time and the opportunity to resolve a problem. We must not doubt that every moment of our reality is of our own creation.

The lack of spiritual progress is often due to a misunderstanding of the principle of causality. This is like a foolish farmer who has a cow and a cart full of grain. When the cow stops pulling the cart, the farmer starts whipping the cart. Do you think the cart will move at all? Under such circumstances, would you whip the cart or prod the cow?

The false I-consciousness is the cause of suffering; conflicting phenomena are the inevitable, dualistic results of the false "I." Now, if you want to change your life, you must deal directly with the false I-consciousness instead of focusing on the body, the environment or the people around you. If you fail to understand the principle of causality, you are like the foolish farmer: Mistaking the results for causes, you are trying to cook sand into rice. The thing to be whipped is the delusion that prevents the recognition of the Pure Mind.

Joshu, the elder, once asked a monk, "How many scrolls of sutra do you read each day?" The monk replied, "Sometimes three, sometimes five." Joshu told him, "You don't know how to read the sutra." Puzzled, the monk asked Joshu, "So, how many sutras do you read a day?" Joshu replied, "One word each day." One is all, and all is one; the myriad phenomena are all verified by just one Mind. The Mind is the source of all problems, but it is also the source into which all problems can be dissolved.

## The Essence of Religion Is Withdrawal

The Venerable Ananda was the Buddha's cousin as well as his attendant. He often had the idea that, being the attendant who took care of the Buddha's daily needs, it was only a matter of time before the Buddha would eventually give him true wisdom. However, after the Buddha's passing Ananda did not obtain the wisdom he had expected. On the contrary, having failed to attain the state of arahantship, he was not eligible to participate in the process of recollecting and documenting the Buddha's teachings.

This experience prompted Ananda to realize that just as intellectual discussion about food cannot satisfy hunger, wisdom cannot come from outside oneself. Only through personal effort can wisdom arise; inaction will bring no result. There is a saying: *"That which comes through the gate is not family treasure; that which dependently arises ultimately will perish."* This very Mind can give rise to all phenomena through the principle of dependent origination, but the nature of the Mind transcends dependent origination because this nature is not dependent on other factors. It is primordially present.

All phenomena are manifested from the empty nature of the essence of the Mind, and they function through the essence of the Mind to assume a dependently arising form. To have the wisdom that transforms our life, one must first change his concept of reality and diligently put that concept into practice. Focus on what you can do right now, and gradually you will have the ability to do what is considered beyond your ability; if you fail to do what can be done at this moment, you will have neither the opportunity nor the ability to go beyond what you are capable of right now. As the story of Ananda shows, karmic results are the concrete manifestations of mind functioning; thus wisdom and merit cannot be obtained from others. One measure of effort brings one measure of harvest; there is neither a God-given Sakymuni nor a naturally born Maitreya.

A common error among spiritual seekers is to imitate the enlightened beings by intellectually grasping their teaching but denying their habitual tendency. This is delusory. The choice of religion does not determine how good a person one is. It is delusory to believe that being a Buddhist, even one with impure motivation, is always better than being a non-believer. A Zen practitioner with impure motivation will not become a better person simply because he or she meditates more. That is another kind of delusion.

Today's spiritual practitioners are often subject to a double standard. On one hand, they cling to the teaching through self-centered I-consciousness with a condescending attitude toward the world, conveniently adopting their own views as the truth and developing a sense of superiority over all others. On the other hand, they rationalize away all personal defects and problems by admitting the failure to attain enlightenment or by abusing the skillful speech of ancient masters with one-sided interpretations. Human beings always choose sides based on personal convenience and benefit, but in this case either side will only further ignorance.

These two sets of standards clash with one another in the

mind of the spiritual seeker, creating conflicts among individuals, organizations, religious sects, religions and nations. They confound the truth to such an extent that human beings lose their sense of direction. Furthermore, some spiritual believers unconsciously hold onto this self-hypnosis as a false view of reality, becoming entrenched in their ignorance of the truth and their extreme rejection of anyone else's perspective. They utterly destroy the message of wisdom and compassion in their own religious tradition as well as its original aspiration to benefit all beings.

The basic intent of religion is to use its teaching to provide a spiritual refuge that guides its followers in life, helping them to eradicate the narrow self and complete their journey toward immortality. It is not intended as a casual or even recreational practice of mind-body cultivation done in a believer's spare time so he can continue to preserve his or her false view of the world. Due to various factors—such as historical evolution, the influence of politics, the economic consideration of religious groups, the messenger's lack of clarity on spiritual essence and the ulterior motive of profit from religion—two sets of guidelines have emerged in the religious community.

One set of guidelines is built on the principle of duality: the reinterpretation of the spiritual message based on the social value of the day, driven by the collective I-consciousness and the shared karma as reflected in today's social structure. This is simply the introduction of the same old worldly game, packaged in a spiritual idea.

The second set of guidelines is a sincere, determined attempt to understand and practice the teaching, though it is still based on the false I-consciousness. Due to the lack of correct guidance in the right view, this approach is often ineffective because the true principle of practice is never fully understood. Great efforts are made, but such efforts are not directed toward the essential task—the destruction of self-attachment, or the eradication of I-consciousness—that reunites the individual with the Collective. Unfortunately, without the right view and guidance, the energy invested contributes to the increase of ignorance and attachment.

Despite their different motivations, both sets of guidelines are created through the phenomena-grasping tendency of the I-consciousness. The former is simply a validation of the rules of the game of *samsara,* the cyclical existence of birth and death, whose foundation is in direct opposition to the essential non-duality of the individual and the Collective. The latter is an attempt to reconnect with the Collective by engaging in the process of restraining the habitual tendencies of the individual. However, it is subject to an unconsciously misdirected effort that actually reinforces the I-consciousness, further cementing one's self-attachment. Concepts such as these, which are based on dualism, will never lead to the ultimate goal of non-duality.

Many traditional religions, as well as today's new breed of spirituality, have inadvertently led their followers onto a path of vague principle and practice in their attempts to reach a broad base of spiritual seekers. By striving to achieve a compromise between the two false views described above and the right view of breaking the attachment of the false "I" in order to attain immortality, many religious groups focus on easily accessible practices that appeal to newcomers at the expense of diluting the true essence and spiritual goal of eliminating self-attachment. Such attempts to actualize Heaven or the Pureland in a dualistic world have forfeited the ultimate goal of immortality and distorted the spiritual essence of the teaching.

Practice based on the direct affirmation of I-consciousness or the motive of breaking through the duality arising from a subtler level of I-consciousness will not accomplish the eternity of life that is the union of the individual with the Collective. In essence as well as intent such practices are based on the phenomena-grasping mind, and are diametrically opposed to the universal truth.

Spiritual practice is the training to eradicate self-attachment by destroying I-consciousness. The withdrawal and reversal of habitual tendencies—right and wrong, the self and others, the subject and the object, and all dualistic confrontations—into the essence of the Mind merges the individual with the Collective, returning the person back to his Creator. Confucianism believes that all human beings can become saints. This is returning humanity to sainthood. Taoism believes that all people can accomplish the Tao, or the Way, and therefore presents a path of returning man toward the Way. Buddhism has taught that all beings can awaken, and this is the path of restraining and withdrawing the ignorance of humanity to allow the pure awakening of Buddhahood.

The ultimate purpose of spiritual practice is the eradication of all false views of reality in order to rediscover the ever-present universal truth, reversing the cycle of form-grasping delusions back toward the primordial, immaculate Mind and withdrawing ignorance into the cosmic ocean of innate awareness. Prayers, meditation, Zen inquiry, recollection of Buddha, recitation of mantra and illumination with mindful awareness are all methods of withdrawal. By the water, under the tree, in a cabin retreat or high in a mountain cave, monastery or temple, with leaves for clothing and plants for food, the arahant without ignorance regarding the right view and the essence of phenomena, the illumination of the mind and the realization of the essence, the rebirth in the Pureland, the Three Insights of One Mind, the Contemplation of the Hua-Yen Mandala, the visualization of Powa (transference of consciousness), Mahamudra the Great Seal, Dzogchen the Great Perfection: these are not distinct from the principle of withdrawing all that is false in order to reveal that which is true.

The universal truth is therefore nothing other than the Mind. The *Diamond Sutra* states, *"If one seeks the Tathagata through form or sound, he is treading a deviant path, unable to see the Tathagata."* The great Way has no distinction of young and old, of different sects, of then and now, of greater and lesser, of east and west or of various forms, but the lesser Way makes the distinctions of young and old, of different sects, of then and now, of greater and lesser, of east and west or of various forms. To fathom the great Way through a deluded mind simply inflates the ego. Spirituality is for the purification of the mind; a pure mind is no longer bound by "I," nor is it fettered by delusion, vexation or attachment.

The opposite of withdrawal is proliferation, or aimless expansion without an ultimate goal. The dualistic pursuit of technology is a form of proliferation, as is grasping at external phenomena. The endless drifting of I-consciousness within its self-made, delusory world is proliferation, and the clash of various beliefs is also a form of proliferation.

Proliferation is the continuation and expansion of the life built on the false concept of "I" which occurs when the individual is afraid of losing his freedom and his "I-dentity" through the process of withdrawal. This is a serious misperception, because unless we withdraw the false I-consciousness and the dualistic world it has created, they will continually bring us suffering.

The individual's sense of separation from the Collective is a delusion. This sense of separation motivates the individual to seek refuge—something on which to depend—by grasping at phenomena that consequently give rise to the vexations of greed, anger and delusion. These feelings lead to the creation of negative karma through killing, stealing and sexual indulgences. The unconscious state of mind is like someone who drifts over the ocean of sentient beings for eternity in a state of amnesia. Any attempt to rediscover the true freedom by relying on one's self-attachment is like trying to build a pagoda in the air; it is ultimately illusory. Only when we, who exist in this world of moment-to-moment change, stop grasping the false "I" and realize our oneness with the Collective can we find true freedom and abide in a state of perfect, natural ease.

Through the union with the Collective, as the Pure Mind, we function in the essence of emptiness without attachment to an independent, isolated existence. When we function this way our existence is instantaneously liberated, and we experience complete freedom. Only in the absence of the construct of "I" can we transcend the limitations of self-imposed identity and attain true freedom.

Most people are afraid that spiritual practice, being a process of withdrawal, will restrict their enjoyment of freedom. But ask yourself: Do you actually have more freedom without spiritual practice? Without spiritual practice are there really fewer limitations in life? If you reflect on this question honestly, it will become apparent that your sense of freedom is simply the delusion of the false self.

The false self constantly seeks refuge in external factors that are always in a state of flux, and therefore it repeatedly loses the sense of existence derived from these unstable phenomena. The insecurity of this delusory isolation continues to motivate the individual to seek new refuge as an attempt to find the next thing that will support this delusory existence. The delusion of "I" has no true refuge, only endless proliferation. This proliferation is the basis of the individual's cyclical existence in life after life.

The common cause of all problems is the inherent instability of the individual's I-consciousness. Because the individual is both the creator and recipient of the results of his karma, he alone is responsible for his problems. They never come from outside. The fact that the individual is experiencing a particular situation is clear evidence that he partakes in the karma and problems associated with that situation. Therefore, he should take responsibility for his share. This is only fair and reasonable.

The mind's functioning will produce corresponding results;

a mind that is focused and pure can manifest clarity and peace. A student once told me that he felt great peace after practicing the *chi-kung* exercise. I asked him whether his mind was still at peace when he was not practicing chi-kung. He answered that it was not. The reason chi-kung brings peace of mind is that the mind has an object of focus and is therefore less disturbed by wandering thoughts. Peace does not come from chi-kung itself; it is the result of a focused mind.

Concentration is the true source of mental calm. Different kinds of mind functioning lead to different energy modalities, which manifest different realms. Different realms imply different forms of existence, and those are the manifestations of various aspects of karma.

If you make a genuine effort in your practice, you will benefit in every aspect of life, and your mind will become clear and subtle. To be a great practitioner you must cultivate diligently like a farmer, paying attention to effort and the results of that effort. If the result does not match your expectation, then re-examine your method of cultivation and renew your effort. This is the attitude of someone who takes responsibility for his reality.

You simply cannot make an effort without paying attention to the results. Logically, you will not have a good harvest unless the right cause and necessary supporting factors are present. A dedicated spiritual practitioner is determined to make sacrifices in his worldly life for the ultimate goal of immortality. When Sakyamuni Buddha took his seat under the Bodhi Tree, he vowed not to rise again until he attained the perfect realization of the Way. The

Buddha vowed to give his life for enlightenment—to sacrifice a lifetime of luxury and prestige in order to destroy the attachment and delusion that obscured the truth. The Buddha destroyed the false I-consciousness and bridged the gap between the individual and the wholeness of reality; he attained liberation from the illusory cycles of birth and death, and actualized the immortal truth that he taught to all beings.

The Buddha is the ideal example of a diligent spiritual farmer. First he planted the seeds for spiritual realization, and then he dedicated his entire life to the cultivation of his spirit, training day and night with diligence. He paved the way of liberation for future practitioners to follow. With the right view and effort, the Buddha attained the goal of his cultivation, the most complete and bountiful harvest. It was, and is, the complete realization of the Way, unsurpassed merit and spiritual attainment, the immortality of liberated activities through the individual, and the eternal purity and indestructibility of the Collective.

Those who do not recognize birth and death busily create karma instead, but those who see birth and death get busy liberating themselves. In life, only one thing deserves our concern: Do we really know the luminous, imperturbable, pure nature of the Mind? There is a Zen saying that goes like this: *"Clobber the delusion until it dies, and resurrect thy true nature."*

Discover the primordial Pure Mind and function from this uncontaminated place; learn all there is to learn and purify all actions so that you can move toward the unborn, undestroyed peace. The unborn, undestroyed peace is the door of liberation for you as an individual, but it is also the display of the completeness and perfection of the Collective. This unborn, undestroyed peace is the true liberation and infinite freedom of immortality.

Not die to the lifeless self, then the immortal nature
cannot come alive;
Not quite alive to the immortal, then one has not
quite died to the lifeless;
To live with what is alive and to die to what is dead
is only half correct,
To die to the living so the dead come to life,
then the world will be at peace.

# 4   A SALTY TASTE IN THE OCEAN

Move image, image moving, image after image arising,

Water waves, waves on water, ripple after ripple born,

Empty the mind, the mind of emptiness, Emptiness just is,

I am aware, aware of "I," "I" after "I" follows on.

Zen is one of many schools in Buddhism. The fundamental tenet of Buddhism is that all beings possess the primordial Buddha Nature; in other words, the minds of sentient beings are essentially pure, having been endowed with the same potentiality for realizing Buddhahood. It is often said that "the Buddha is a sentient being without vexation, but the ordinary being is a Buddha with vexation." The deeper message is that, through diligent effort, each individual can eradicate his attachments, purify his mind and thereby attain Buddhahood.

Another fundamental concept of Buddhism is that the primordial Pure Mind—also called the Awakening Mind or Buddha Nature—is always present through a sentient being's transmigration from one life to the next, from one incarnation to another. Although the individual has created the delusory I-consciousness, he remains inseparable from the Pure Mind. Regardless of the specific time and circumstances in which the individual manifests his or her existence, the individual cannot be separated from the Pure Mind, just as the shadow cannot be separated from the constant, all-illuminating sun.

However deluded an individual's existence might be, that existence is momentary, arising and dissolving instantly and simultaneously. Due to the unconscious nature of the false "I," the illusion of independent existence is maintained. This very sense of independent existence is the outwardly grasping tendency; a baseless and deluded discrimination that must be eradicated through Zen training.

Zen Master Bai-Yun Sho-Duan once said, "*That which transforms phenomena is the Tathagata—like the warmth of spring, the mountain flowers blossoming everywhere. Possessing the hands of inexhaustible manifestation, without ever changing the original face, the dramatic performances continue on.*" The past was it, the present is it, the future will be it: the Buddha Nature possessed by all beings.

## Self-Attachment Distorts the Truth

The term "mundane" refers to the sensory realm, the world and the existence of phenomena. The mind of a mundane person is contaminated by self-centered narrow-mindedness. A mundane person is attached to the sensory world and trapped in the cyclical manifestation of phenomena, unable to extricate himself from the limitations of space and time. In other words, he is a prisoner in the dungeon of phenomena and is unable to find a way out. A mundane person is someone who handles reality through his false I-consciousness, attachments, judgments, delusions and habitual mental tendencies; he has not yet recognized the true nature of the Pure Mind.

What is the difference between the mundane person's mind and the Pure Mind? What is the difference between the mind contaminated by false I-consciousness and the non-dualistic, selfless Pure Mind? In Zen, it is customary to use the analogy of a perfectly clean, clear mirror to demonstrate the essence and function of the Pure Mind. When a mundane person's mind functions, it is similar to a dusty, stained mirror that is unable to reflect an image clearly. In much the same way, a mind that is contaminated by the dust of self-attachment will always distort the manifestation of the truth.

Attachment obscures the original clarity of the Mind. It twists and distorts our ability to perceive reality's true presentation and use it as the basis for our interaction with the environment and acquisition of knowledge. But if the mirror is clear and immaculate, it will accurately reflect reality's true form much like the Pure Mind, which is free of self-attachment, bias and judgment, delusion and habitual thoughts.

A completely enlightened person directly perceives the source of life, the Pure Mind, and the non-dualistic union of the individual and the Collective. In the context of Zen, "the Mind is the Buddha" and "each thought is a sentient being." Thought arises from the Mind, and only the Mind can give rise to thought. All beings are manifested from the Buddha Nature, and therefore the Buddha Nature is the only true refuge for all beings. From the reference point of the Buddha Nature, all beings arise from the Buddha Nature, and the Buddha Nature is inseparable from beings. And from the perspective of beings, all beings' existence is based on the Buddha Nature, having been born from this Buddha Nature.

Given the perspective that all beings arise from the Buddha Nature, it can be said that all beings have the Buddha Nature. Because no functioning is possible without the essence, all functioning must arise from it; no single being can be separated from the Buddha Nature. Because all beings must arise from the functioning of the essence, or the Buddha Nature, it is said that all beings must also possess it. Without essence, there is no being.

The source of thought is the Mind, and the source of beings is the Buddha Nature. Free of deluded thoughts, the Mind manifests; free of ignorance, the Buddha Nature is revealed. Thoughts and the Mind are inseparable, but thoughts are already liberated in themselves. Beings and the Buddha Nature are inseparable, but all beings are actually liberated. The one who is enlightened is able to give rise to thoughts from the essence of the Mind, and thus the individual functions based on the Collective.

While the individual functions, moment to moment, each thought remains connected to its source in the essence of the Mind. Each thought dissolves into its primordial nature, as the functioning individual, changing from moment to moment, abides in the refuge of the Pure Mind of the Collective. Therefore, it was said: "Upon seeing, one acts. Once acted, put it aside. Thus done, what else is still unfinished?"

The Pure Mind is formless but always present. It is the True Self, which is one of the four virtues of the Mahayana conception of nirvana: *permanence*, *bliss*, *self* and *purity*. The True Self, however, is not the self produced by attachment to our thoughts and body. The True Self is not the false, independent sense of individualism; it is the selfless Self, the universal refuge of withdrawal from all phenomena, the creative source of all individuals, the omniscient and the all-encompassing entity, which is neither inside nor outside. The True Self is timeless; the Pure Mind of the True Self is emptiness, luminosity and clarity. It is what the Zen masters referred to as the tree without a shadow, the permanent foundation without roots.

An enlightened being functions without attachment through his primordial nature, creating undefiled causes and results. The mundane person, however, is unable to function this way. He functions through the delusion of self-attachment that arises from the ground of the primordial nature; through the deluded I-consciousness that lacks awareness of the truth.

Because the mundane person cannot give rise to phenomena and thoughts with awareness of the essential nature of the Mind, he creates the subject-object duality by separating the "I" that grasps phenomena from the phenomena being grasped. Because the mundane person has no recognition of the common root of life and the reality of existence, he never realizes that the subject and object—the actor and the acted upon-- are nothing other than simultaneous, inseparable manifestations of the Mind, the source of all things.

The sense of independent existence drives us to chase after phenomena, and in the process creates confusion regarding the truth. We lose touch with the essential emptiness and awareness of the Mind, and instead our mind functions through self-attachment. The mundane person fails to realize that no individual or situation can ever transcend the Mind, which is the Collective. In other words, he does not realize that outside the Mind there are no phenomena. In this lack of understanding, this delusion, the false I-consciousness is born. He does not realize that outside phenomena there is no Mind, and therefore he is unable to manifest the Pure Mind of the Collective. The Mind is the phenomena, and the phenomena is the Mind. The Mind and phenomena are inseparable and non-dualistic. The differences between the enlightened and the unenlightened are vast and all-encompassing: purity and contamination, truth and delusion, the real and the fictitious, selfless and self-centered functioning.

All beings are lost in ignorance due to the defilement of the false I-consciousness, but all sentient beings, whether enlightened or not, possess the Mind. An ordinary being, under the veil of ignorance, is never for a moment able to separate himself from ignorance, unconsciousness, right and wrong, the self and others, judgments, and distinctions of the inner and the outer, nor is he able to separate from attachment and deluded fantasies. Through the false self he has defiled, fragmented and restricted the selfless True Mind of the Collective, which is as vast as the Great Void.

The spiritual practitioner strives to attain the state of realization, the direct recognition of the selfless, pure and complete perfection of the Mind. He seeks to experience the splendid realm of Hua-Yang, no longer perplexed by the contradictive definitions and doctrinal divisions of various spiritual traditions. Zen Master Hung-Chih Cheng-Chüeh advised his disciples as follows: "*Bright moon above, reeds over the foggy water, sail forward like an arrow piercing the chilling light; having personally arrived in Lu-Lin to inquire the price of rice, then one is qualified to open his mouth.*" Only through the transformative experience of enlightenment can we realize the truth: All is inseparable from the Mind. Only transformed by this realization are we then qualified to speak the truth.

Those who have recognized and become able to function completely from the Pure Mind are called the Enlightened Ones or the Accomplished Saints, and each has mastered his own mind and life. For these beings, at all times, under all circumstances, function arises and dissolves instantaneously without attachment and confusion, always in union with the Collective. The Collective functions through the individual; the individual perceives the Collective as a refuge. The relationship between the individual and the collective is non-dualistic and inseparable.

Enlightened beings can function through the innate Pure Mind of the Collective, able to manifest the various individual and myriad phenomena in life. They also have the ability to open manifold realms of phenomena at will in order to resonate with different beings and benefit them. Such an enlightened being can function in the direction of his intention and experience its influence on reality.

The saints do not succumb to confusion within the experiential sphere of phenomena, but instead abide at ease in the awakened nature of the essence. Since they already see reality as it is, they mindfully give rise to pure, wholesome karma that benefits all beings without the side effects that accompany delusional judgments. The goal of Zen training is to clear the attachment that arises from the I-consciousness. Eradicating attachment allows each individual to actualize the immortal luminosity of tranquility. This is the eternity of Heaven and earth, where it is possible to experience the clarity and vast openness of the Mind of the Enlightened Ones, to breathe

the same breath as the ancient patriarchs.

We shall explore in greater detail the practical methods of breaking attachments and attaining enlightenment, but first let us consider the apparent contradiction of the so-called "constraints" and "freedom" in the reality of life. Take the case of an ancient culture with thousands of years of custom and tradition. A group of individuals living under a particular cultural umbrella, with its deep-seated, structured thinking, necessarily develops a unique, collective personality—the artifact of that cultural construct. This inherited collective personality will undoubtedly impose some limitation on the behavior and psyche of the group.

By contrast, a country without a long history of cultural tradition does not have deep roots in a particular set of customs and traditions and is more likely to put forth new ideas and an alternative social structure. Without a strong cultural background, the limitations of the group's pattern of thinking are minimized, and the rapid development of multicultural values and structures becomes possible. But the pitfall of rapid development is the lack of stability. A new society, unstable and divergent in direction, is less likely to form an integrated point of reference for consensus-building.

The integration of multiple ethnicities requires both time and an integrating concept. This concept must provide a reference point that overcomes the individualistic, divergent tendency of the society and provides withdrawal. Without this reference point for withdrawal, different social and ethnic groups will distance themselves from one another through mutual respect and the attempt to tolerate their inherent incompatibility. Without the concept of spiritual withdrawal this distance cannot be bridged, regardless of the time given to the process. For countries and cultures with deep historical roots, those roots become a form of limitation.

A flexible mind is more adept at absorbing and digesting new concepts, regardless of whether their impact is positive or negative. If the mind is already filled with concepts and beliefs, the habitual tendencies of the mind will attempt to filter and discriminate any new idea that is presented and will trigger reactions as the mind attempts to bridge the old and the new.

Take the following koan: A student paid a visit to an enlightened Zen master and asked, "What does the Mind look like?" The master replied, "If I told you the truth, you would not believe me." The student said, "Master, of course I would believe you." So the master said, "The Pure Mind is like a giant beast with three heads, many arms and legs, and extreme ugliness."

The student was very surprised by that response because, according to his understanding of the sutra, the Mind should be formless, all-pervasive in the universe and able to manifest all existence. So, he said to the master, "What you said is the wrong answer!" The master replied, "As I tried to warn you, if I told you the truth, you would not believe me. Beating the drum in front of your face, you still do not see. The question you ought to ask is why you cannot recognize the present reality."

There is a Zen phrase, "missing what is in plain sight." The Zen master tried to give the student a hint of reality based on his direct experiential knowledge of the truth. The master showed him the truth by cutting off his thought so that he could finally turn the mind inward. Unfortunately, the student's grip on delusion was strong, and he continued to indulge in the falsehood of imagination. An individual who is filled with opinionated thoughts will experience great difficulty illuminating his own nature in order to recognize the truth.

The tendency of the I-consciousness to grasp external conditions is called "dualistic thinking"; it is the way of functioning that separates the subject and object. As you read this page, without any conscious intent on your part, pre-existing concepts in your mind filter its content. The text describes the emergence of dualistic distinction, and you are employing the ideas that you have already understood as the basis for interpreting the meaning of this description. But, regardless of what you believed or understood, and regardless of how broadly you are able to relate to this idea, everything remains within the confines of the false I-consciousness. In fact, at this very moment you are using the perception and view of the false "I" to comprehend the meaning of this text.

Based on the I-consciousness, you have applied a definition on top of what I attempt to express. Your definition comes from you, but my expression comes from me. In other words, there is no direct connection between the concepts arising from your I-consciousness and the real concept and view that I have tried to express. It is the delusion of the individual to force a connection between your view and my view as true understanding.

The individual's view of reality and the truth of existential reality are two different answers. This, in essence, is duality. Dualism and the confrontations arising from it are the sources of all human conflicts. Every individual tries to understand reality through a colored perception, experience and pattern of thinking established by the false I-consciousness. This refraction causes a single reality to manifest as many different perceptions and understandings. When we are obsessed with our own view, conflict naturally arises and we are unable to resolve our disparities with others. A life with a burdened framework of thinking isolates us from the truth. Any attempt to understand reality through such a limited framework of thinking is a game for the ignorant. It is the self-deception of fools.

A mind without the fallacy of I-consciousness manifests the truth. Such a mind, like an untainted mirror, is the Pure Mind. However, to see the truth through the self-attachment creates a dualistic conflict. It is similar to two persons wearing glasses of different colors, one red and one green: The world they see will also be different. To one the world is colored red, but to the other it is green. Both possess the same capacity to see, but they speak of different worlds because of a distorted perception of the world as seen through the colored lenses.

When our understanding of the Collective is distorted by the I-consciousness, our view is the illusion of a deluded consciousness. Ironically, the illusion presented by habitual tendencies—the only means by which an unenlightened being is able to perceive the world—becomes invariably and inexorably both his attachment and his truth. Conflicts between individuals, societies, countries, religions and ethnic groups are the unavoidable results of this dualistic world.

Human beings are dependent on external phenomena, continually seeking and craving satisfaction from phenomena. Through analysis and reasoning, man strives to discover the governing principle of reality in order to stabilize the world of phenomena, and this motivates the pursuit and development of dualistic thinking. But any phenomenon is a passive manifestation, a function and a presentation of the Collective. Thus the presentation of phenomena is actually an indivisible Collective emerging from the cross-penetration and support of multiple space-time dimensions of reality. One-sided opinions and self-centered perceptions, and the conflict that they cause, are deluded attempts to fragment this indivisible Collective.

### The Mind's Functioning Manifests Karma

Imagine that alien beings have arrived on earth with the sole mission of selecting a religion that represents the truth and bringing it back to benefit their home planet. Without a preconceived notion about earth or a preference for any particular religion, a conference with the leaders of all the world's religions is held. In this conference, each leader presents his religion with great passion and conviction, being ready and willing to put his life on the line to assure the extraterrestrial visitor that his religion represents the truth, as supported by case after case of personal testimony. After listening to all the testimonies, the only sure conclusion—and the only evident fact—the alien beings are able to discover is that every human being possesses the ability to believe in what he believes in, to create a reality that dependently arises from his belief, and to live a life within the reality he or she has created.

The individual creates, at each moment, the only result he is capable of creating through self-attachment. He has no choice but to accept and rely on the result he has created and to stubbornly believe it is right. With this *modus operandi*, human beings create various karmic distinctions, such as race, belief, wealth, poverty and social status. This *modus operandi* has no exception; only that which is without exception can be the universal truth. History has no lack of examples in which individuals or groups, in the name of upholding the truth, have engaged in acts of aggression against one another in the form of political, religious or ethnically discriminatory war. These are not the faults of the universe, the gods or the Buddhas; they are the consequences of individuals acting under the influence of delusion.

An individual creates and follows his beliefs, acts according to them, obtains the corresponding results and then attempts to coerce everyone else into conforming with those beliefs. This pattern applies to all aspects of life. The individual accepts only his own definitions of reality and becomes habituated to describing his reality through those definitions. Such definitions are not the truth, but are simply his personal theories. Universal truth has no exception; it is the principle that is universally applicable and that which no individual, situation or existence can transcend.

The Mind can give rise to any thought, and the corresponding phenomena will simultaneously manifest in reality. Therefore, the Mind creates and manifests all phenomena; no existence can transcend the Mind. It can give rise to a limitless variety of thoughts, and different mind functioning will generate different brain waves, each with its own energy composition. The appearance of thought is the presentation of energy.

When a joyful thought arises, the whole body will experience comfort and our facial expression will change. Our hormones, muscles and even the environment can be affected. When the Mind functions, all aspects of phenomenal manifestation occur simultaneously, with-out the distinction of first or last. From the standpoint of the individual, all forms of existence manifest instantly, in a cohesive wholeness of multi-faceted manifestations. This is the so-called moment-by-moment manifestation of the non-dualistic Collective.

It is stated in *The Mind-King*:

> *The salty taste in water,*
> *The gel and color in paint,*
> *Their existences are certain yet formless,*
> *The Mind-King is just so.*
> *Abiding in the body at times,*
> *Coming and going through the sense faculties,*
> *Responding to objects and following the senses,*
> *Free of obstructions and completely at ease,*
> *Accomplishing all endeavors.*

Create thoughts and functioning through the Mind, and the entire realm of phenomena shall instantly respond in mutual reverberation and manifest in each moment of reality. The Mind's functioning triggers a rippling effect in the infinite dimensionality of the phenomenal world and pervades all existence; as a result, the body, environment, relationship and phenomenal world are simultaneously and equally impacted by every thought in each moment. The mind's functioning has the power to effect changes in phenomena.

Since the phenomenal realm changes with the individual's mind functioning, each thought impacts all aspects of life. The inexpert use of the mind and its functions can harm others and ourselves, and can negatively affect one's life as a whole. For example, an angry thought is linked to the phenomenon of anger, and anger has an immediate functional impact on the individual and his relationship to the environment. It is essential that we understand this concept.

The real problem for the individual is that he most often fails to realize that he is continually, from moment to moment, grasping external phenomena with his mind functioning, oblivious to why such thoughts have come and where they have originated. From the moment we awaken in the morning to the moment we fall asleep at night, we generate countless delusory thoughts, but such thoughts represent only an extremely small fraction of our awareness or what is deemed important. Generally, our speech, actions and experience of daily life occur unconsciously.

The mundane individual unconsciously creates his present and future karma, as he can only unconsciously create thoughts. Unconsciously he depends on them and makes use of them, only to be surprised by the results of his mind's creation. This pattern leads human beings to manifest reality unconsciously and live with the unsatisfactory results. Without self-awakening, the same kind of karma is continually repeated. This is why life is filled with difficulties and a sense of helplessness.

## The Mind Is the First Cause of Life

The essence of the Mind is formless but able to function. The moment this formless Mind functions, each thought is distinct, an independent function arising and dissolving instantaneously. The moment a thought arises, if the mind is unable to abide in the formless essence of innate awareness, it simply grasps that thought and unconsciously identifies with it as "I," furthering the development of a false sense of self. Because the nature of thought is independent—each thought is unique from any other—the attachment that grasps thought as "I" or the self automatically inherits a sense of independence as well. This is how an individual acquires a deluded sense of independent consciousness.

The Mind is formless but is able to create and manifest all phenomena. If the Mind does not give rise to a mind function of feeling, there is no feeling. If there is not a mind function of seeing, we look without seeing. If we do not give rise to a mind function of hearing, we listen without hearing. Our mind functioning sets the direction in which phenomena are manifested, but different thoughts come with different feelings. When the Mind's function stops, everything ceases in the absence of feeling and thought.

Even when people possess sense faculties, in order to experience the world they must give rise to mind functions of various sense faculties. This demonstrates that there is something behind the senses and something is allowing the sense faculties to function. That which causes the sense faculties to function is the true source, the true master. Thoughts, feelings and phenomena simply result from the functioning of this source.

Medical equipment may be able to detect the brain waves or energy associated with thoughts, but they cannot detect the source of such phenomena. The source is the Mind, which is the source of all mental and physical phenomena, even though it remains formless, in a non-energy, non-material state. Physical science and technology may detect only a small portion of the functions of the Mind, but they cannot provide a true understanding of the emptiness and luminous characteristics of the Mind. It is the source of all phenomena.

The relationship among phenomena is extremely complex. The material phenomenon of the present moment is merely a fragment of the entirety of phenomena encompassed by the Mind. The material phenomena that existed in a different time and space comprise only a portion of the collective phenomenal whole encompassed by the Mind in this present moment.

Although the myriad of phenomena are interrelated, their relationship is not a causal one. A single instance of the material existence of phenomena can neither create nor cause another instance of material existence to come into being. An attempt to detect phenomena with equipment can only capture the degree of interaction that can be quantitatively measured between the equipment—which is a material phenomenon—and the phenomena to be measured. But these highly constrained and incomplete measurements are often presented as evidence of the source of some manifestation or the cause of a certain problem. This is a serious error based on the idea that a result can give birth to another result, instead of the principle of a cause giving rise to the result.

Only relationships, not causality, can exist between results. Most medical and scientific knowledge, however, is deduced from the relationships between phenomena that are results, without seeing and understanding the true source of phenomena and reality. The true cause of phenomena—in other words, the "first cause" of everything—is the selfless, formless essence of the Mind. With the formless essence of the Mind as the cause, through the mind's functioning all phenomena are manifested as the results.

The truth of the Mind can only be recognized by the enlightened saints. Without true understanding of this first cause, any amount of theoretical development and speculation only promotes further misunderstanding and misleads in regard to the karma of sentient beings. Developments or speculations along these lines will always fail to resolve the difficulty that humanity faces.

Man lives his life based on his own ideas and definition of reality, and he interacts with situations based on the unconscious pattern of mind functioning. To label someone as "bad" is simply the reaction of the unconscious mental pattern toward that person. In truth that person is just as he is. An individual's thinking is not that of God, nor is it the view of the Buddha. Good, bad, right, wrong, correct and incorrect are superfluous definitions that ordinary beings assign to phenomena, according to different geographies, cultures and karmas. These definitions do not possess real meaning; they are merely the rules of a worldly game that changes according to circumstantial factors, such as the people involved, the time and the place. Due to their subjectivity, these definitions will not lead to recognition and certainty regarding the truth.

Buddhism refers to human beings as sentient beings, which are beings with mental activity or signs of life, such as brain waves. In contrast, a wooden Buddha statue is not a sentient being. It does not possess attributes of life, nor can it think because it lacks mental activity and brain waves. Since Buddha statues are only material, not living organisms, why do so many Buddhists visit temples or monasteries and prostrate and pray to them?

People have endowed these Buddha statues with a definition that associates the object with the quality of magnificence and holiness, so that it becomes natural to react to the presence of Buddha statues with a respectful mental attitude. People apply the definition of holiness and sanctity to the Buddha statues and react according to that definition. In other words, a person uses his own definition to uplift his spirituality. The truth, however, is that regardless of what we think of these Buddha statues, they are simply lifeless objects. They have neither emotion nor mental activity.

The mundane individual creates self-centered attachment through the delusion of an independent consciousness; he builds up unconscious mental and behavioral patterns that respond to people, situations and objects in a very modular fashion. Functioning in life according to this modular set of reactions, he creates certain results. Reality is therefore subject to the definition of the individual's particular mode of mind functioning.

The Buddha taught that with the emergence of the Mind's function, phenomenon arises; with the cessation of the Mind's function, phenomenon ceases. As the Mind's function transforms, the world of phenomena is transformed; as each function of the Mind differs, the world of phenomena also differs, since the Mind is Buddha. Knowing this principle, we can naturally liberate ourselves from vexation. To uplift and improve our life, we must understand the unconscious pattern of mind functioning that has only existed in the mind of the individual and was created by the core state of consciousness of our own definition of "I."

In his state of ignorance, man has long mistaken his habitually self-centered thoughts as the true self and confused the function of the Mind to be its essence. The functioning of the Mind is infinite, but the individual has become dependent on the functioning of the attached mind and drifts aimlessly in the ocean of delusion. It is as if someone were taking the son for the father and turning the truth upside-down. This delusion is the beginning of the endless mistakes and suffering of life.

Spiritual practice is a lesson in the mastery of life. The master of life is the Mind; the phenomena of life are the results of the Mind's functioning as they emerge from the Mind's essential nature. Everything is a functional extension of the Mind, which encompasses every definition and mental concept. When the accumulated tendencies of the false I-consciousness solidify into habitual patterns, life becomes dominated by various should's and must's and loses its innate freedom and purity. The individual creates and reinforces his definitions and patterns through continuously using those patterns to interact with the environment.

Earth is now home to 6.7 billion people, which means there are at least 6.7 billion different possible ways of mind functioning. Our way is merely one of them. Our minds have become so limited, and we are utterly disqualified from making any claim of correctness in our own view of reality. Still, we see no alternative but to go on living based on our narrow way of thinking. It is no wonder that we are so easily entrapped by difficult situations.

The mind is infinite in its function, but its capacity has become restricted by habit. This is comparable to a toddler who, despite having only a few words in his vocabulary, tries to understand the world through the few words he recognizes. Because we are unable to control the habits that create repetitive thoughts, it is difficult to transform our circumstances. This trap results in the difficult situation in which life's vitality and freedom are helplessly depleted. Like a boat drifting aimlessly in a vast ocean of karma, life is a drag without energy and freedom. We suffer until the last breath of our present life, which is only to be followed by a similar predicament in the next life.

## The Mind, the Most Effective Factory

A mind that lacks awareness is the critical cause of life's problems. This lack of awareness is due to an intensely forceful self-attachment, the grasping of the false, independent consciousness as "I." This lack of awareness refers to a deluded mind that functions without awareness concerning the essence of the Mind. Delusion regarding the Mind's essence leads to the delusion of the mind-induced, but any thought that lacks awareness regarding the essence of the Mind is a delusion.

In truth, the essence of the Mind is an emptiness in which functions arise and dissolve instantaneously. All the while there is not even the temporary presence of an unchanging "I," an objectified, concrete selfhood. Nevertheless, due to our attachment to the notion of "I" based on a false, preconceived notion of independent consciousness, an unchanging "I-dentity" is created.

The deluded individual functions with an unconscious state of mind. Zen refers to such unconscious mental activities as the "lone lamp under the sun." The functioning of a deluded mind lacks awareness, so the very notion of independence of the individual is a delusion that violates the universal truth of emptiness and impermanence. To maintain this false sense of independence, the individual thinks and acts for the fulfillment of the self. Consequently, with this false self as the cause, he creates a rigid set of habitual thinking and personality, which becomes his "second nature."

Like the skin attached to the body, habitual thinking follows the individual everywhere so that the individual becomes his thoughts. These habitual thoughts then occupy the individual's mind until they become the only thing he possesses.

To give up on these thoughts, we lose our sense of direction in life, but by using these habituated thoughts, our life will remain closely confined. Such is man's self-made dilemma. The power of habituation is very strong in its ability to direct our thoughts. Therefore, an equally strong measure of self-awareness—awareness without the tendency to grasp at phenomena—is needed to counteract and change our habits.

We must start by recognizing the unconscious, deluded thoughts that arise in the mind. It is very important that we have the ability to observe our habitual mental activities. Without that ability we will live unconsciously, oblivious to why certain thoughts and actions occur, and we will allow them to continue poisoning the mind.

The Mind is the greatest, most powerful factory in the universe, and it is capable of producing an infinite array of thoughts and phenomena. However, the ordinary person's mind has become extremely limited. Such a mind is enslaved by habitual thoughts and illusions that give rise to stubborn and unconstructive thoughts, and unconsciously he chases after these thoughts. Like the blind and the dead, the ordinary person drifts unconsciously along with his habitual thoughts, unable to see the right direction or hear the true sounds. He is ignorant of the truth, the essence, the function and the dependent emergence of life.

Confined by his present situation and unable to liberate himself, the ordinary person becomes entrenched in a rigid pattern of thinking. Unconsciously attached to a habitual mode of mind functioning, he has forgotten the fact that his factory possesses unlimited potential. While in possession of this, the greatest mind factory in the universe, the ordinary being continues to manufacture flawed products of low quality day after day, year after year, through negligence and poor management, until the end, when his life is at last exhausted. The sad truth is, the Mind is the most wasted natural resource in this world.

Most people only recognize and use a minuscule portion of the Mind's enormous capacity. This is because each individual has unnecessarily narrowed himself to the notion of "I," and that perspective unconsciously gives rise to thoughts that grasp at phenomena. The grasping of phenomena is an ongoing, unconscious mental process. Even during sleep, the mind continues to entertain thoughts as they emerge from our karma, as well as the experiences and encounters that have occurred during the day. The hallucinations, nightmares and insomnia we experience are ample testament to the fact that the mind remains in a state of restlessness while the body appears to be asleep.

The life of an individual who has many delusional thoughts is filled with hesitation and restlessness, because a deluded mind cannot find a path toward the peace of the Pure Mind. The mind is always active—unconsciously creating thoughts of varying degrees of attachment in response to external attractions and unconsciously giving rise to a series of habitual thoughts. It is a ceaseless process.

One thought always leads to another; so each thought has no chance of dissolving back to its true nature, or its true home. Attachments and discriminations reduce the capacity of the mind; the unconscious mode of mind functioning is a person's bondage. The purpose of Zen training is to release the structure of attachment and I-consciousness and liberate the individual. Following the Buddha's instruction and example, each practitioner strives for enlightenment and liberation from suffering in this lifetime, in order to extricate himself from the cycle of birth and death. If we do not liberate ourselves in this lifetime, in which future life do we plan to do so?

## "To Say It Resembles Something Misses the Point"

Fourteen hundred years ago, the Sixth Patriarch of Zen, Master Hui-Neng of the Tung dynasty, revolutionized Zen by transplanting it as a uniquely Chinese spiritual tradition. One day a practitioner, Hui-Rang, came to visit Hui-Neng. Hui-Neng asked him, "Where do you come from?" Hui-Rang replied, "From Mt. Sung." This is a typical question that Zen masters employed as a means of examining a disciple's state of realization and understanding in regard to the nature of the Mind.

Most any person would take this question in the literal sense and respond by giving the name of his hometown or where he had lived. However, to a Zen practitioner this is the most subtle type of examination, because only a truly enlightened being is able to answer adequately. Imagine yourself standing in front of me and hearing me ask, "Where do you come from?" You might answer "Ohio" or "New York." But pondering this answer further, the "you" in this moment of inquiry is hundreds of miles away from Ohio; the "you" in Ohio is not here right now; nor is the future "you" standing before me. However, the "you" in Ohio is not "other than you"; the future "you" is not separable from the present you.

The function of the Mind is inseparable from its essence. Do you understand that now? If you understand, then say so; or if you don't, just say so. If you can say something, this one utterance gives birth to a new life, but if you can't respond to it you have died right here under this very question. Since you are in front of me, why do you say you are from Ohio?

Life occurs in every moment and in each individual, as expressed in the function of the Mind and the Collective, which are non-dualistic. The essence is formless but is manifested in the individual according to various factors and conditions. The individual and the circumstances in which he is situated are the embodiments of this very Mind; they are just dependently arising phenomena without a concrete "I." Outside this present moment, everything else is merely an illusion of the individual's propensity to grasp at phenomena.

The Mind expresses itself through the dependent emergence

of phenomena from the Mind's emptiness in this present moment. Outside the present moment, there is no expression of this essence of the Mind. Specifically, the instant of mind functioning that arises from the mind essence is the present moment, and within this dependent arising realm of phenomena there are the so-called individual and his corresponding surrounding conditions. Together they form the one and only Collective, the non-dualistic composite in which the mind function and its essence are inseparable. Only an enlightened being is able to realize this point.

The functioning of the Mind is always in a state of flux. Thoughts and the environment change from moment to moment, and all existence is subject to constant change. From a medical perspective, the body is the aggregation of cells, but cells do not possess the ability to initiate change. However, the composition of cells is subject to change. The body changes due to differences in the composition of elements; even mountains and rivers are subject to change. In reality, thought appears and vanishes instantaneously. Each thought is momentary, unique and independent in the sense that there is no causal relationship. The thought from a previous moment cannot cause change in the thought arising in the present moment; similarly, the thought in the present moment cannot cause change in the thought arising in the next moment. The notion of change simply refers to the fact that the thought from the previous moment is different than the thought in the next moment.

The real question is as follows: Who is changing the thought, the body and the environment? Because thoughts are independent and cannot affect one another, in this physical body there is no such thing as a tangible "I" that can cause thoughts to change. All functions arise from the emptiness of the Pure Mind, which is the reason that the question, "Where do you come from?" stands at the gateway of spirituality. If you can directly experience the real source, the point of origin for all life's activities, you will then know how to respond to this question.

The false I-consciousness causes the individual to stubbornly hold onto his self-centered ideas, treating the false as the true. When Hui-Rang responded to the question, "Where do you come from?" with "From Mt. Sung," it is clear that he was stating his last stop. Is this answer wrong? The issue is that his life—the true person who was functioning with the Mind in that very moment—did not come from Mt. Sung. Therefore, Mt. Sung was not the source of his existence.

Hui-Neng then asked, "What is it? How does it come?" What was Master Hui-Neng really asking? In this instant, your mind's functioning is manifested through the act of reading this book. This is the only reality. Life is always just this present moment: the direct instance of the Pure Mind's expression. This present moment is not the same as the common notion of "now." "Now" is a concept relative to the notion of a past and future, though it is still defined in terms of phenomena.

The individual grasps changing phenomena as his basis for understanding phenomena, and due to the change in phenomena the notions of the now, as well as the past and future, are born. Attachment is the attempt to stand on an absolute, unchanging reference point of observation. However, no observer who stays in a fixed position can observe all phenomena, nor can the observer actually choose what to observe; the observable phenomena are already present upon the very instance of the observer's appearance. The observer and the observed both arise and dissolve simultaneously, while the subject and object unite.

The individual always observes phenomena through the absolute reference point of his self-attachment. Any notion of the past being discussed in the context of the present moment is still the past relative to the present moment, not the real past; and any notion of the future discussed in the context of the present moment is still the future relative to the present moment, not the actual future. The manifestation of the Mind in this very moment is the only reality; it is the individual's only true possession.

What actually follows you, once you leave a place? Only this very Mind! Wherever a person is, the Mind is there; and wherever phenomena are manifested, the Mind is there. The Mind is the root of all phenomena, because it is the True Self. There is a Zen saying: *"When it's cold, the whole universe is cold; when it's hot, the whole universe is hot. Just let it be."* The moment the Mind functions, phenomena manifest instantaneously without any boundary or separation. The Mind is not separate from the Buddha, nor is the essence separate from the function; the subject and object are one. When the Mind is not functioning, in the tranquility of no thought there is just the true emptiness and formlessness of the Mind. When the Mind functions, all activity is complete and perfect.

The moment thought arises, the observer and the observed simultaneously emerge. Therefore, in the ultimate sense there is no such thing as an independent, objective observer outside the phenomena being observed, because the observer is already a part of the phenomenon. It is a fallacy to try to establish a reference point for observation upon another phenomenon, since one phenomenon cannot observe another.

Because Hui-Rang was not yet enlightened, he could not respond to Master Hui-Neng. His mind was dependent on phenomena, so he could only respond by saying, "from Mt. Sung." In Zen, only the present moment matters, because it focuses on the direct experience of the present moment, rather than on mental speculation or unconsciousness. Only the direct, experiential present moment is real, and in this moment the formless Pure Mind is functioning. The conceptual idea of time—the now, the past and the future—is merely a delusion arising from the mind that grasps phenomena.

Hui-Rang attained enlightenment after eight years of study with Master Hui-Neng as his attendant. Later he recalled their initial encounter, saying to Master Hui-Neng: "Hui-Rang now understands the words you spoke when we first met." The Sixth Patriarch then said, "So, how do you understand it?" Hui-Rang responded, "*To say it resembles something misses the point.*" The Sixth Patriarch then asked, "*Can it still be cultivated?*" Hui-Rang said, "*If it can be cultivated, then it is not emptiness; if it can be contaminated, then it is unattainable.*" At this point, Hui-Rang had the penetrative insight into the formless nature of the Mind, so he authentically responded to Master Hui-Neng's subtle question. From this response, Master Hui-Neng recognized the enlightenment of Hui-Rang, that he had seen the True Mind and reality. With this verse Master Hui-Neng confirmed it: "*Just this uncontaminated is blessed by the Buddha; thus it is for you, thus it is for me."*

The sole aim of all paths of spiritual practice is to realize the Mind's essential nature. Only the essence can be cultivated and realized. Everything else is dependent-arising and subject to dissolution. Thus it is said that "the Great Wall still stands today, but Emperor Ching is unseen," and "The three realms of existence are like a house afire." All beings possess the innate Buddha Nature and are capable of awakening, but the purity of the Mind has been obscured by the false self, including unconscious thoughts, discriminations, biases and beliefs. If the individual can diligently engage in the correct Zen practice and break from attachment, enlightenment will be assured. Having the right view in spiritual practice, it is only a matter of time and effort. Once enlightened, the individual understands that nothing surpasses the Mind. The Mind is All, as the Mind is the universe. Outside this Mind there are no phenomena, and outside the phenomena one cannot find the Mind. Therefore, he is able to be completely at ease under any circumstance. This is true liberation. This is Zen.

> Soldiers guarding the border at the order
> of an ignorant emperor,
> Holding their ground with determination and bloodshed;
> Guns ring and the sound of thunderous explosions
> filling the sky,
> Killing one another, not recognizing that all belonged
> to the same clan.

# 5    THE SELF AT EASE

Turn over the bed in the monk's quarters,

Puncture the fantasy, the stars in the eyes;

Amusing samsara in his palm,

Golden Ox dances away.

"Give me liberty, or give me death" is a well-known slogan. In history one finds many dramatic tales of individuals who fought for independence and freedom, as well as in various discussions on what freedom means to people. One can talk about freedom for a country or freedom of the individual, but in a broken nest there are no undamaged eggs. So, without the freedom of the Collective, individual freedom is impossible.

For most people, freedom means achieving a certain degree of material and emotional fulfillment according to their wishes. The Zen perspective on freedom stems from the Pure Mind, because the Pure Mind is the entirety of phenomena, the Collective. Since the Collective is by nature liberated—due to the characteristics of emptiness, formlessness and selflessness—the freedom of the Collective is assured on the level of the essence. However, if the freedom of the Collective were to depend on other conditions—in other words, if liberation were not an innate quality—then even in the union of the individual with the Collective there would be no freedom.

Regardless of the type of freedom we consider, if the individual or the Collective is not already free in essential nature, any pursuit of freedom will be futile, and any resulting appearance of freedom will simply be a relative, deluded sense of freedom. Only when liberation is already inherent in the essence can liberation be obtained. This is done simply by expressing our nature.

The functioning of the individual and all the corresponding phenomena arising from the Pure Mind are on the level of the essence, which is already free and liberated. Because the essence—the source of phenomena—is by nature liberated and free, the functions arising from this source also possess the characteristic of freedom. From the perspective of Zen, freedom simply means the non-dualistic union of the individual and the Collective, in which life is a completely liberated state of perfect ease without attachment.

## Freedom of Zen

The freedom of Zen has two aspects. The first is the freedom of essence, the complete liberation from one's habitual definition of self and the unconscious mind functioning that arises from it. This aspect allows the manifestation of the emptiness, awareness and luminosity of the Pure Mind. The second aspect is the freedom of functioning, or the ability to freely function through the mind, which opens up the dharma realm and its myriad phenomena without the false conceptions of subject, object, beings and time. Freely functioning through the mind, we are able to enter and exit dharma realms in an unhindered manner. The freedom of Zen has many levels, but to find this freedom we must use some method to extricate ourselves from the unconscious bondage of the mind.

A Zen saying goes like this: "*This old body wears a cotton coat, plain rice fills the belly, sewing patches to fend off the cold, everything unfolds and completes as it should be.*" The Poet Bai wrote, "*The luxuriant flowers had vanished by April, as the peach had just begun to blossom in the mountain temple; lamenting the spring had gone, nowhere to be found, man does not realize to turn inwardly here.*" These two poems provide a glimpse of the freedom of Zen, but it is different from the ordinary notion of freedom. The ordinary notion of freedom implies the absence of responsibilities and obstacles; the opposite of that condition is the suffering that arises from responsibilities and obstacles. In other words, any form of restraint or limitation, whether material or spiritual, is defined as a lack of freedom. But the freedom of Zen is the absence of vexation and a sense of perfect ease, regardless of one's external circumstances.

Many believe they have freedom as long as they can do what they want, dress the way they like and say what they want to say. In the reality of life, this level of freedom is difficult to attain. Perhaps such freedom is possible under certain supporting circumstances, but it will also vanish when those circumstances change. In other words, circumstantial freedom is not true freedom. From the perspective of Zen, such freedom is a dependent, relative form of freedom; it only occurs under certain conditions.

The reality is that such a relative freedom is hard to come by. Just the lack of money to purchase something desirable is a kind of obstacle to fulfilling our wish and sense of freedom. Real life is full of examples in which things fail to happen the way we expect despite the enormous effort invested, or in which we are overwhelmed by afflictive emotions that cannot be stopped no matter how deeply we desire to feel otherwise. Afflictive emotions and troubled situations create a sense of stagnation, deficiency and powerlessness about life, not to mention a lack of freedom.

Consider the practical limitations of daily living. We need a job, some form of transportation, a phone for communicating with family, hygiene to maintain health, pure water to drink, clean air to breath, food to nourish the body, shelter for protection, and money. Still, many people in the world today cannot even obtain those basic necessities. When needs and desires are not fulfilled, there is naturally a sense of suffering and the loss of freedom. If we contemplate the present conditions in our lives, it should be clear that trying to attain relative freedom is difficult because we are already living under the limitations and bondage of our desires.

How can we obtain true freedom today? If we have a family, a job, certain social obligations and other practical matters to handle, how can we live our life with a sense of independence and freedom? If the essence of the Mind is dependent—that is, unable to stand alone—then we will never find true freedom. Dependency can only produce relative freedom, not true freedom.

Because the conditions that support our sense of freedom are changing, such freedom is inherently unstable, short-lived and unreliable. Most people, in their pursuit of relative freedom—whether listening to the music they like, engaging in activities they enjoy or seeking comfort in the company of certain friends—believe they are enjoying true freedom. But in truth, they are unconsciously cultivating dependency on conditions. Becoming attached to these conditions, the individual sets up internal conflict between his desire to seek true freedom and his attachment to the relative freedom he has created.

Zen teaches us to enjoy favorable circumstances while they last and accept adverse circumstances without mental hindrances. When the mind remains at ease under all circumstances and experiences, the individual is in possession of true freedom. Zen Master Seng-Zhao, just before his execution, said: "*The Four Elements had no owner, the Five Aggregates were originally empty; meeting the blade with the head, just like cutting the spring breeze.*"

Able to transcend life and death, a truly great capacity of the heart and real freedom is gained. Therefore, under all circumstances we should train to maintain a clear, peaceful mind. Through sustained practice that polishes away the rough edges of our mental conditioning, the tranquility, peace, purity and "not birth, not death" nature of the Mind will be revealed. True freedom is the manifestation of the "not birth, not death" nature of the Mind.

Nirvana, or the transcendence of birth and death, is the ultimate state of functioning according to the universal principle. The self and the universe are inseparable from one another, and the self is inseparable from emptiness and phenomenon. Being inseparable from emptiness, the self is liberated and at ease, thereby attaining the universal freedom. Inseparable from phenomena, the individual's manifestation merges with the Collective as a non-dualistic oneness. All is the self, and the Collective is inseparable from the individual; the self is inseparable from all, and the individual is inseparable from the Collective. Emptiness and phenomena are as one, and essence, function and phenomenon are as one. The primordial, ultimately liberated characteristic of the dharma realm comes forth as the great nirvana, great liberation, great ease, countless nirmanakaya, and the great freedom of entering and exiting dharma realms. This is the ultimate, true freedom.

## Liberation Matters to Everyone

A long time ago, a good man died and met the King of Hell, awaiting judgment. The King of Hell asked him, "Since you have performed much charity and lived a life of goodness, in the next life you shall return to the human realm. Now, please tell me what kind of life you would like to have." The man said:

*A high government official as a father,*
*To the honor of first place in imperial examination my son shall attain;*
*With thousands of hectares of fine, fertile land surrounding my home,*
*Abundant with barley and rice in my barn;*
*My treasure chests are also full of silk, silver and gold,*
*Fish pond, flowers and various fruits grow in my garden;*
*Virtuous are my beautiful concubines and charming wife,*
*To the highest level of nobility shall I be born, and*
*Enjoying fortune and glory, and live past a century.*

The King of Hell, after listening to his description, said, "If what you want is possible in the human realm, I will be happy to go through reincarnation for you!"

We inevitably encounter troubling situations in life, so none of us can claim, "I can achieve the satisfaction of all my desires and needs, and enjoy complete freedom, ease and happiness." This is impossible in life, because the individual has many attachments that necessarily lead to obstacles and suffering. Depending on external circumstances, the individual is unable to recognize what true freedom is and thus commits his entire life's energy to the pursuit of things outside himself to stabilize his sense of false self and comfort, and to secure a measure of relative freedom. The basic human needs are simple: food, air, clothes to keep warm, and the safety of shelter. Having met these needs, the human being, begins to seek the meaning of life and true freedom.

Modern man, even though his basic needs are simple, believes his needs far exceed these and therefore wants even more. The availability of technology provides the conditions and factors that support relative freedom, feeding man's dependency and desires. This situation leads to the proliferation of deluded thoughts and the discovery that even more is needed to sustain the relative freedom of deluded thoughts.

The more needs are created in order to sustain relative freedom, the less "free" such freedom becomes. It is a degenerative cycle. Like Kua-fu, the giant of ancient Chinese mythology who tried to chase down the sun, or like traveling in the vast void of space without an end destination, man must first realize the futility of pursuing materialism as a means for human happiness before he can abandon his dualistic concepts.

Only through restraint and withdrawal from habitual tendencies can man find true satisfaction and freedom; otherwise, technological advancement and material abundance will only add to man's confused focus in meeting the needs of his delusion, creating even more relative freedom with limitations. The mind that seeks external phenomena for stability is on a path of no return that only leads to countless contradictions, conflicts and vexations. Humanity, being led down the path of a materialistic culture by the collective consciousness, has created today's highly developed technological society. The cost is the furthering of the collective ignorance that steers humanity away from the true Mind and innate wisdom.

Many people believe liberation is a Buddhist idea, something only Buddhists care about. If they are not Buddhists, it is unrelated to them. Worse than this attitude is the view that liberation is a form of suicidal self-termination. The fundamental meaning of liberation is the eradication of suffering and the attainment of happiness, not the ending of life out of despair. Whether mundane or spiritual, whether an individual is practicing or not, mental vexation is the greatest obstacle to a fulfilled life and the eventual attainment of the Way. Zen practice must involve the concept of liberation, and the effort to attain liberation is crucial.

We must learn how to liberate ourselves from the attachment of unhealthy mentality and habits. Before thinking about attaining complete freedom and perfect ease, which are as vast as the ocean and boundless as the sky, we must first have the ability to abide in our essential nature so we can resolve the conflicts in our present life's situations and attain happiness.

If a practitioner fails to recognize that worldly happiness and the attainment of spiritual realization are simply different scenes along the same path, he will split his practice from the reality of life and create contradictions that cannot be resolved. Being unable to get any benefit from his practice, he will come up short on both sides. Many practitioners fail to recognize that the spiritual and the worldly are two facets of the same truth; without the correct understanding, their practice is stagnant, lacking in vigor and commitment.

Human beings interpret everything based on their past experience, applying their understanding of the past to new concepts. For example, right now the thoughts that arise in your mind while reading these words are the only ones you can have at this point in time and space. Because they are based on the old ideas and beliefs that have long occupied your mind and governed its thinking, they hinder its ability to absorb new ideas. New ideas are interpreted through past experiences, so the mind continues to operate under its old pattern, which makes it difficult to learn and change.

Liberation, from the common perspective, is difficult to obtain when our life is based on an outdated pattern of thinking. This is because our daily behavior and mode of interaction with people and situations are based on habitual tendencies. Because human beings spend their entire lifetimes creating, cultivating and unconsciously imprinting certain habits in the mind, these patterns have completely defined the individual: who he is, what he knows, and what he is capable of doing and experiencing.

Because the mind has become occupied by these imprints and attachments, it necessarily excludes new experiences that are different. This incompatibility is the result of duality, where conflict and restlessness begin. But, if we are able to liberate the mind from the self-centered definition of reality and its habitual tendencies, then the selfless Pure Mind becomes manifest. When we can release the mind from the bondage of inner attachment and the cycle of birth and death, the powerful expression of our true self begins.

Reincarnation is very important as a basic concept of spiritual practice. When the individual cannot release his dependency on the I-consciousness, this sense of false independence prevents him from experiencing non-dualistic unity with the Collective, or the Pure Mind. To be imprisoned by the conceit of "I" and unable to escape its repetitive patterns of functioning is to be subject to reincarnation. Reincarnation can be thought of as slavery in chains, because the individual's activities are bound within a certain space with no prospect of freedom regardless of any labor or effort. Before attaining enlightenment and liberation, the individual is enslaved by the false I-consciousness.

Under different manifestations of space-time phenomena, the I-consciousness undergoes constant change. In the reality of habitual thinking, the I-consciousness takes on different roles—the oppressor and the oppressed, the murderer and the victim, the action and the reaction—and engages in the exchange of energy based on the law of causality. Through this process, the individual continuously assumes opposing roles within the dualistic reality created by the force of his karma. The repetitive creation of mistakes and role exchange manifest as the cycling of a complex web of relationships and interactions. Based on the self-centered habitual tendencies, the individual reacts to phenomena in a predictable, repetitive manner, perpetually producing similar situations. This cycle is also a form of reincarnation.

The functioning of the I-consciousness has no essence outside the realm of phenomena, nor does it have any awareness outside the realm of phenomena. Because the I-consciousness depends on phenomena in order to give rise to thoughts, once the phenomenon-grasping thoughts cease, the individual feels a loss of identity. Only in the instance of grasping phenomena is the ordinary being able to derive a sense of self by identifying with his deluded thoughts. With-out phenomena and the support of a succession of delusory thoughts, the individual loses his dependency and the feeling of existence.

The consciousness of ordinary beings cannot transcend phenomena; they cannot see past form or hear beyond the sound. The functioning of I-consciousness—its creation, existence and reason for being—is completely based on phenomena. Just as the *Surangama Sutra* states, *"If apart from the previous sense object there is still a discriminating nature, then that would be your true mind. However, if the essence of this discriminating is nonexistent apart from the previous sense object, then it is nothing but a shadowy manifestation of the mental discrimination of the previous sense object."*

An ordinary being's selective awareness is based on the delusion of the I-consciousness instead of the true, pure awareness of the Mind. This capacity to discriminate dissipates with the dissolution of sensory objects and lacks essence in itself. Ordinary human beings have been conditioned to grasp phenomena, and they are are unable to define the True Mind. Consequently, they are unable to employ its full potential. It is for the purpose of regaining intimacy with our nature and its full capacity that we engage in Zen training. Can you, at this moment, take full mastery of your own thoughts?

A simple test will show whether you can have the thoughts you want: Please close your eyes and relax the body. Breathe naturally. Without giving rise to other thoughts, focus your attention on the inhalation and the exhalation. After five minutes or so, open your eyes and recall. Were you able to focus completely on observing the breaths? Were you able to stop all thoughts by focusing the mind? If you can, then in a certain respect you are the master of your own thoughts and are able to control the functioning of your mind.

Mind functioning is the key that opens many of life's channels; different mind functioning creates the divergent paths of the holy and the ordinary. Through self-attachment and the grasping of phenomena, the ordinary is made, and through the selflessness of the Pure Mind—illuminating the emptiness, suchness, truth and the innate awakening of our essence—the path to sainthood is paved.

The Mind is like water that can either give a ship buoyancy or sink it. When we have the ability to generate the thoughts we desire, we are able to bring forth the life we want. When we lack mastery over our mind, we become the victim of our own mind functioning. Most people spend life—meaning time, energy and resources—compensating for the undesirable consequences of the thoughts and actions their deluded I-consciousness directed. As most people waste their lives in this manner, this is a very serious problem.

The Mind has unlimited capacity and potential. Its functioning is the most powerful and intricate of all organized operations. Man, due to his ignorance of how to utilize the Mind, has diminished the potential and power of his own mind. Although ignorant of the truth of life and only vaguely appreciative of the power of the mind, man nonetheless appears satisfied with the substandard results of life that he has obtained. Under the control of self-attachment and habitual tendencies, he sails across the turbulent sea of desire, with delusion and craving as the sail and the false I-consciousness as the rudder but no compass to guide him to shore. Without the light of guidance, sentient beings continue to wander in confusion, lacking direction and refuge. Only by breaking through his attachment can the individual sail toward the light and security.

The greatest flaw of an individual in life is the inability to recognize his own paralyzed thinking pattern. As a result, he remains stagnant. The individual self-righteously holds onto his deluded I-consciousness as he gives rise to mind functions, not just once or twice but repetitively creating the same thoughts of attachment that lead to the same depressed, futile predicaments. The ordinary being is either unaware of his life's real situation or is still in denial of it. A student once asked me, "Should I be a wise but suffering person who knows his own problem, or should I be an ignorant, happy-go-lucky piglet?" This question demonstrates that many people are not willing to face the real self, or the real life.

The Mind is capable of manifesting any circumstances we desire. Lacking control, however, the ordinary being cannot avoid encountering certain thoughts, and constantly tries to overcome the unpleasant circumstances that repeatedly occur. Unconsciously, he creates more karma and habitual tendencies that lead to further deterioration in the future. Without awakening to life's painful truth, we have no choice but indefinitely prolonged suffering. If the reality of our everyday life holds confusion, discord and the sustained experiences of similar phenomena of conflict, this is reincarnation.

Man, as if in a rat race, lives his life in a repetitive cycle of unpleasant situations where his efforts continually push him back to where he was before. Thus, satisfactory results are never achieved. He will continue to create karma unconsciously and then become attached to the phenomenal manifestation of karma instead of looking toward the source of the karma, returning to the Pure Mind.

Habitual tendency determines the direction in which our karma is manifested as reality. It is the hand—the force—that turns the wheel of birth and death. The unconscious mode of mind functioning propels man in this endless cycle of birth, aging, illness and death. Only with liberation through the enlightenment of our true nature can this vicious cycle be broken.

Reincarnation is the most disheartening condition of existence, because it is filled with nothing but suffering. To stop the wheel of suffering, we must begin the work from this present moment and practice giving rise to a single, mindful thought. Each of us possesses this primordial Mind that can generate thoughts and direct our life's destiny.

Take this to heart and endeavor accordingly, and your life can be changed for the better. There is no need to fear death: It is only the act of casting off the physical body, which is merely the transitory phenomena arising and dissolving according to the law of dependent origination. The True Mind's emptiness and clarity, however, are eternal and deathless.

The True Mind is formless and eternal, both manifesting and encompassing the individual's karma in each single moment. Only the totality of manifestations represents the wholeness of the True Self. If an individual wants to spend time worrying about something, let him be concerned with just one thing: He has not yet mastered the mind; he is not yet a true owner of the Mind's great capacity. If the individual is unable to mindfully manifest the thoughts that establish wholesome, desirable karma, then he must be feeding the mind with poisonous thoughts. The results of this thinking will be more suffering that will follow and torment him in every life. This is the most dreadful truth: a never-ending horror movie that features the individual as its main character and victim.

A commitment to Zen training and the correct application of its principle in our daily life, however, make it possible to achieve liberation from the grip of self-centered confusion and vexations. Perseverance in our practice ensures the realization of the True Mind, which brings about a complete, permanent release from the cyclical existence. This release is the goal of Zen training, as well as the result it guarantees.

Through correct practice, the benefit of Zen training improves all situations and all aspects of life, including physical health, relationships and livelihood. The individual will also awaken to the fact that various vexations, apprehensions and the fear of death are dream-like illusions that are ultimately unsubstantiated and cannot come to pass. Therefore, he is able to freely engage this world of suffering and enjoy the freedom of "thus attaining in the unattained."

Generations of Zen masters, after attaining the realization of the Way, have attempted to liberate beings through various skillful means. While some masters employ unusual behaviors and styles of teaching, their conduct is always for the purpose of teaching all beings the universal truth that they have realized. They are no longer attached to false I-consciousness but are able to express the universal truth in every action.

Take the famous koan known as "Golden Ox, Rice Bucket."

Each day, just before the noon meal, the monk known as Golden Ox would dance in front of the dining hall with a rice bucket, laughing out loud, "Bodhisattvas! Come eat!" This went on for twenty years. If the purpose was to announce the arrival of meal time, hitting the gong or the wooden fish would suffice, so why bother with the dancing and the spectacle? The skillful means deployed by masters are for no other reason than to help each student take direct responsibility for himself, reminding him of the commitment to seek the realization of the truth of birth and death for himself, in every moment of the day and with each single thought.

Many Zen masters have left us with verses related to this koan. Master Xuedou said, "*Laughing out loud in the shadow of white clouds, with both hands it is given; if thou are the true son of Golden-Haired Lion the Awakened One, three thousand leagues away you can already see through the failed display.*" Master Foyan said, "*Fox dung all over the monk's bed, the dog barking in front of the Three Saints Hall; leaping out of Golden Ox's nesting cave, the bright moon illuminating the night travelers.*" The patriarchs spare nothing to awaken the disciples; this is the act of a true bodhisattva, not a display of insanity or deceptive dramatization.

Enlightenment, the perception of the path of the universal principle, is the goal toward which all Zen practitioners strive. The principle indicates a direction; to understand the direction of life and how it operates is to be enlightened to the Way. The Way is the universal principle that governs the operation of the phenomenal world. The Way is primordially liberated as it transcends existence. To be enlightened to the Way, or to actualize the Way, liberates the individual and reveals the universal truth.

Man creates everything in his present moment of reality. Before attaining liberation, his life remains bound by the totality of his mental imprints. Only when there is freedom from the habitual definition of life's path and reality can we create, at will, the desired life and environment. To a great extent, our present life is directly impacted by our past or previous life. The term "past life" refers to the countless existences that maintain some degree of connection to the phenomena of this present moment.

The so-called past is the aggregation of a vast, incalculable number of factors and conditions from the entirety of space and time. For the sake of brevity, we refer to the collection of these factors and conditions as the past life. Based on the aggregation of an incalculable number of factors and conditions in the present moment, those manifestations that share resemblances to the present karma are called the future. More precisely, the most frequent habitual mental and behavioral consequences of the past will have the strongest influence on the reality of the present lifetime.

Each moment of life is intimately connected to all aspects of one's existence. Due to man's ignorance, the existence in the moment is taken to be concrete and independent. This ignorant interpretation casts the moment into the fictitious framework of space and time. The self-centered attachment becomes the "I" as the subject, and the objectified, independent phenomena becomes the "person," or the object.

Objectifying phenomena inevitably leads to the notion of spatial occupancy, from which the concept of space is born. When the objectified phenomenon is perceived as moving from one space into another—so that, from the reference point of self-attachment, the objectified phenomenon appears to be moving—that movement requires time. Consequently, the concept of time is born.

Self-attachment is essentially the notion of self; it is the false I-consciousness or the belief in a concrete, unchanging self. When there is self-attachment, it follows that there must be an observer situated at the absolute reference point, and that such observer perceives all phenomena. The observed phenomena are the notions of person and beings. The observer's concept of an individual lifespan, as well as the movement, change and disappearance of phenomenon, depends on the notion of a time span, or the notion of time.

A different existence can be distinguished in terms of energy: When thoughts arise, the corresponding energy emerges. Thought is energy; in the moment of emergence, its energy draws out a space in the Void. This thought is connected to countless dimensions in which the energy of similar characteristics is present layer upon layer, composing the existence of phenomena that resonate with the thought. The energy of the thought itself is only a very small portion of the Collective but is intimately connected to the limitless energy behind all existence.

Phenomena differ from one another as a result of the variations in the composition of their energy. For example, the body cannot move alone, because movement must be accompanied by a related thought. Otherwise, nothing will happen. All things in life are intimately connected to thought. Life is therefore the extension of our mind functioning, therefore the mastery of our mind functioning means the mastery of our life and the ability to influence the entire phenomenal realm. This is the universal truth.

As the Mind functions, the thought instantaneously connects with the entire world of phenomena and becomes manifest in the Mind. Outside the Mind, however, there is no phenomenon. The physical body, relationship, environment, universe and the manifold realms of phenomena are all images projected by the Mind. No matter how subtle a certain mind functioning is, it immediately and directly impacts life. This is one of the most subtle principles, and it shows how life's reality is formulated and presented.

The various modes of mind functioning develop into the core around which life evolves. Mind functioning is intimately connected to the phenomenal existence of the Collective: who I am, what I will encounter each day, and who I will become in the future. Because thought and karma are closely linked, life's unfolding is determined by the pattern of mind functioning. In other words, the pattern in which thoughts are created determines the form and state of existence of various sentient beings. Without conscious control over the pattern of mind functioning, thoughts and behaviors repetitively and unconsciously occur, ensuring the continuation of the wheel of reincarnation. The individual in this unconscious cycle will encounter the same problems and relive a similar quality of life, molding and shaping his future circumstances and conditions, life after life. This is a most serious matter.

The most important thing in life is the mind's functioning pattern. This is the deciding factor in our quality of life and the fruition of spiritual practice. Countless thoughts are unconsciously created each day, and each thought has the power to impact our health and environment, as well as the universe and all existence. The strength of attachment will influence the density and intensity of the reality created, the phenomenal manifestation and the phenomenal realm. The function and strength of thought have control over the energetic composition through which phenomena materialize.

The repetitive creation of similar thought, and therefore energy, reinforces the thought and accumulates strength. For example, negative thought is a main cause of disease. The process from the initial cause to the manifestation of symptoms of a physical disorder is driven by the same negative thought, as the minuscule amount of energy in thought accumulates into a concrete physical symptom. It is only through the repetition of the same thought that it becomes strengthened. Once it is sufficiently powerful, the manifestation of energy that resonates with the karmic frequency of human existence becomes the symptom experienced by the individual.

The evolution from the initial cause to the eventual maturation of a physical illness is essentially the layered composition of energy. This composition of energy is induced by thoughts of varying strength, intensity and function. The dynamics of all phenomena progress unconsciously. In terms of energy, the seed of the illness has long been planted unconsciously and developed over time into a full-blown symptom that exists outside the individual's awareness.

Through the process of repetitive thinking, the individual body and life undergo changes. Ultimately, once the accumulated power of the thought reaches a critical point and condensation, pain and illness are manifested. Mind functioning can lead our life into different situations, and it will cause various health conditions. We are the sole creators of our own life: our own body, the entire universe and all existence.

Zen training is learning to master our mind and thoughts. Without the ability to consciously command the process of thought generation, life will not unfold according to our expectations. Many people have the *"I am in charge of my life"* illusion, but in reality that control is very difficult to obtain. Spiritual practice, from the Zen perspective, is liberation from the habitual, uncontrollable thought process and the breaking down of the mental molding of the I-consciousness, in order to reach the state of true freedom.

The most important goal in Zen training is the attainment of enlightenment. Awakening to the Mind's innate awareness and destroying the self-made bondage of the false "I," we can live in complete harmony with the essential nature of the True Mind. There are various degrees of enlightenment, and the depth of our realization could be compared to the brightness of the moon during different phases in its monthly cycle. Although the nature of the light is the same, the brightness and expansiveness vary, ranging from the initial state of realization to the complete enlightenment of Buddhahood. When the state of complete realization is attained, ignorance is uprooted without residue, and we enjoy total freedom in how we function through the Mind.

The sages who perfected the actualization of the Way had the ability to manifest at will in different phenomenal realms. This is neither a fantasy nor a myth. It is a fact. In the historical records of Buddhism, many practitioners demonstrated their complete mastery of the Mind. If we want to cultivate this same ability, the first task is to recognize our habitual thoughts, dualistic ideas and self-attachments, and then eradicate them through the diligent application of correct methods that ultimately lead to liberation.

The practice of Zen is for the purpose of finding the Pure Mind within us. Liberation is not really about freeing ourselves from another's control; instead, it is about liberation from the false self. Having released our mind from delusion, confusion and attachment to habitual thinking, the cycle of birth and death will come to an end. The vexation and burden of mundane existence will be eradicated, and all aspects of our life will be uplifted.

Once the innate Pure Mind is rediscovered, we can directly experience the wholeness of reality in the functioning of the Pure Mind. In the light of truth—the inseparability of self and others—we learn to become the master of our own life. Just as the *Diamond Sutra* stated: "*The bodhisattva shall abide in suchness, and subdue mental delusions in suchness,*" eradicating the cycle of reincarnation, we freely choose our role and form of existence as we practice and gradually perfect the Way of the Bodhisattva. This is the ultimate purpose and state of attainment in Zen training. Once there is complete understanding of this path, there is nothing more worthy of pursuit than to be life's true master.

> From the depth of spiritual abode comes
> the sound of the bell,
> Empty valley listens by itself without a person;
> Rainbow leading the way toward the Tusita Heaven,
> Auspicious, lotus-like clouds veil all tracks of movement.

# 6 LIVELY SPIRIT

Blind touching the elephant, nothing like the elephant,

Image in the broken mirror, no longer true;

Speculating, wondering, running in circles,

Turn around and touch the Self, then the true "elephant" is found.


Accomplished practitioners, as well as practitioners in denial of reality, try to focus their lives on spiritual cultivation. While diligent practice is critical, what is easily overlooked is the manner in which the practitioner handles the problems of daily life. This is the true test of his practice; it is the deciding factor in the effectiveness of his effort. The ordeal of life is directly connected to the individual's karma, and the focal point of a practitioner's learning is to apply his spiritual attainment while facing the challenges in each moment of his life.

If the same issue repeatedly plagues a practitioner's life but he stubbornly tries to ignore it by focusing only on a spiritual concept and practice, it is simply the avoidance of reality. Actually, it is ignorant to focus solely on practice and allow suffering to continue while failing to heed the troubling aspects of one's life in order to eliminate obstacles. Life's problem is the mind's problem, which is manifested in every instance according to the principle of causality. A true spiritual practitioner cannot postpone the resolution of these issues waiting for rebirth in some Pureland or in Heaven. If his view and actions are otherwise, he will continue to remain in this world of defilement.

Human existence is characterized by the mixture of the wholesome and the unwholesome, or positive and negative karmas, which makes it impossible to experience complete fulfillment in life. Before we realize the Pure Mind, it is still necessary to use the relative wisdom of our ego to manage life's affairs and promote positive development while minimizing the negative side effects. The principle of action and reaction tells us that all dualistic functioning must bring forth repercussions. The philosophical basis of this principle is founded on the dualistic separation of the subject and object. If, in each moment of life, there is the attachment to "I" as the agent of action, as well as an opposing object, the individual will always function from this point of reference. Each action toward that object creates another reaction upon the "I."

In the dualistic world, any benefit must come with some harm. It is only a matter of degree. The reality of life is that in harm there is some benefit and in benefit there is some harm to be found. When handling daily affairs in this world of duality, the unenlightened individual should adopt the principle of "weighing on the side of more benefit and less harm." He should strive to separate himself from his attachment to phenomena, learn to live with equanimity in both favorable and stressful situations, and employ each adversity as an opportunity to recognize and eradicate self-attachment.

Adverse conditions may look like something external to us, but in reality they are the results of our own inner defilement. Without arousing our inner awareness and then calming the mental agitation, there is no basis upon which to transform the so-called adverse external conditions. For that reason, we should engage in training to cultivate the ability to destroy attachment in daily life and cultivate a lively, spirited mind, content and at peace under all circumstances. Only through this approach can we be free of the need to complain, which only aggravates suffering. Instead, we will have the mental calm and clarity needed to create a better future.

## Different Thought, Different Channel

According to the law of impermanence, all things are in a state of flux. Thoughts will change, and the body, environment, people, situations and seasons change constantly as well. To have a mind that is lively and flexible, we must learn to live with impermanence. Everyone wants favorable circumstances to last forever and unfavorable circumstances to vanish quickly. This is not merely a contradictory perspective but also an impractical one, since it violates the principle of impermanence.

Self-attachment makes us wish for change in external circumstances instead of within ourselves. It seems convenient to assign fault to an external situation and succumb to the false self, but it is a path of no return. Lacking the initiative to make change, how can we actually expect the outer circumstances to be any different than what they already are? All obstacles and troubles are our own business. Without change, problems will be unresolved. No progress can be made as long as we remain in this world of impermanence.

The solution, when life does not unfold as we wish, lies in correcting the course of change. Life is impermanent, regardless of whether or not we agree. It is a law of nature that human beings will constantly change. Thus the question is whether we can remain awake amid the impermanence of phenomena. Can we employ impermanence to our advantage? What is the direction in which we should point our life, given the inevitability of change? Is the desired direction of change possible, and do we have the ability to make that change? What outcome will that change produce? In life, people come and go, thoughts come and go, emotions fluctuate constantly and the body is ever-changing. Change is continuous in each moment. Objects and situations appear and disappear, while phenomena and conditions arise and fade away. In Zen, this is the so-called "dust." Given a world of continuing change, only one thing is certain: the Mind, or the Source of Life. The Mind is innate and eternally present; it does not vanish after the dissolution of the physical body. Layman Fu explained this idea with a poem: *"Certain Substance comes before Heaven and Earth, formless and at perfect peace; master of all phenomena it is, never degenerating with the changing seasons."* The Mind is the master of everything, while ideas, emotions, thoughts and phenomena are products of the Mind, its servants and shadows. Unfortunately, ordinary beings treat the servant as the master and follow its orders, treading the divergent path at its command.

The stubbornness of human behavior is strong as a ship anchored by the rope of attachment. Unless we can untie the knot at the end of the rope, the ship will remain stuck no matter how much effort is made to set sail. *"Myriad karmic manifestations all differ, lifelong labor gives no ground for escape."* If we cannot transform ourselves, all effort simply turns into the fatigue of a cyclical birth and death.

The practitioner should bear in mind that every event in his reality corresponds to the Collective Life. In other words, his thought at this very moment, as well as everything else—every situation, person and circumstance encompassed by the Mind—directly corresponds to the Collective. The moment that thought arises, like the rippling of water, it invokes manifestation from the infinite potential of the Mind, which permeates all dimensions of space.

The functioning of the Mind is *not*, contrary to what most have traditionally believed, conducted through thoughts. Thought is *not* the causal agent of change, but instead thought is that which is produced or transformed. It is the product of the Mind. Within an instance of the Mind's functioning, both thought and its corresponding phenomena simultaneously become manifest. All phenomenal existence is the direct manifestation of the Mind's functioning; only for the sake of simplification is it said that changing thought will change phenomena. What actually occurs is that the change of thought is the result of different functioning of the Mind, and therefore the change of thought is only part of the result due to the different functioning of the Mind. Due to the change in the functioning of the Mind, there is a change in the form of existence related to the energy level of the thought.

Thought and phenomena arise and dissolve simultaneously, not one before the other. All phenomena, including thought, are encompassed by the Mind and born from the Mind, which is *whole and wholly inclusive*. Thoughts and the infinite number of related forms of existence are merely symbolic of the Mind's creation, being the result of the Mind's function. We are exclusively responsible for every encounter in our life. We are the sole owner of our life, and all the joy, grief, suffering, relationships and situations are of our creation. To change life, we must change how we function with our mind; only then will outside relationships and situations change.

The Mind's functioning is similar to a radio: If the reception has noise due to interference, we must change the station. Once the radio signal resonates with a clear incoming station, the interference will disappear. To complain about the brand of the radio, the quality of the programs or the weak signal from the towers will have no practical meaning in terms of the situation. Solving a problem is like listening to a radio broadcast: When life is filled with noise and interference, we must change the station. Instead of adjusting the frequency of their reality, most people just complain; they continue to suffer without any improvement in the situation.

Let us consider the story of a traditional Chinese puppet show: An elderly man becomes captivated by the storyline of a puppet show on television. Each time the hero is sabotaged by the antagonist, the man becomes outraged. One day, in a bout of anger, he tosses the TV into the sea and vows never to watch the show again. However, when the time for the show arrives the next day, he still wants to see it. So, he has no choice but to go to his neighbor's home, once again to be angered by the antagonist.

This story shows that if we focus only on the surface aspect of a problem, the mind's thoughts will continue to cling to the problem. Such a state of mind lacks clarity. Even if we are able to reach some meaningful conclusion after pondering a problem, it must be followed up by concrete action in order to find a resolution. To solve a problem, we must first recognize and stop the unconscious mode of mind functioning that has become intertwined with the problem, so that the mind can give rise to new ways of functioning. Most people, obsessed with ideas of their own individualism, are unable to function from within the Pure Mind. The individual is the one who falsely believes in his independent, isolated existence within the present situations and conditions and, as a result, unconsciously severs his connection to the wholeness of life.

Man, who is attached to the idea of individualism, pursues phenomena and holds on tightly to them through the functioning of his mind. It has been said, "Man chases phenomena in ignorance; the phenomena chases man who has awakened." Ordinary beings always try to suppress phenomena by habitually grasping at phenomena. This is similar to rolling a snowball down a hill while trying to solve the problem of a growing snowball. It is self-defeating. If we wisely use the methods of Zen training to calm the craving for phenomena, the mind will instead become clear, able to perceive the root cause of a problem and, wisely, achieve a different level of functioning in order to resolve the problem.

## Impermanence Is a Mixed Blessing

It is easy to find examples that demonstrate the fragility of relationships between spouse, children, relatives and colleagues. Disturbing emotions such as anger, jealousy, competitiveness, pride and greed are hidden threats to these fragile relationships, which are delicately maintained. Man spends nearly his entire lifetime trying to juggle many hidden threats as he maintains various relationships, and he suffers greatly because of it. Relationships dissolve and resurrect repeatedly until the individual, numb and bereft of hope, eventually becomes resigned to the situation.

It is impossible to maintain the delicate balances in human relationships for very long. The real way to a long-term solution is to change the focus of the relationship and cultivate merit in order to resolve the hidden factors underlying the fragility of relationships. The individuals in the relationship should make a combined effort to uplift themselves spiritually and let go of attachments. Then, and only then, will there be less friction and greater acceptance and practical wisdom in dealing with the challenges of daily life.

Only the Pure Mind can manifest wisdom, and only through wisdom can we perceive the true source of problems as attachment in the mind. Consequently, the only way to cultivate greater capacity and tolerance is to loosen our self-attachment and break down prejudices. A mind of great capacity and wisdom is the prerequisite for dissolving the problem that is hidden behind the delicate and fragile balances within a relationship and creating a manner of interacting that is truly harmonious and wholesome. The only true path of resolution is to cultivate inner awareness and address problems at their source, since any other effort will only temporarily stabilize the checks and balances in a relationship that is subject to collapse any moment.

The individual is composed of impermanent factors, so a relationship between individuals is impermanent. The core of the individual—his false sense of "I"—is inflexible, while the basis of the relationship between two individuals changes constantly. A problem in any relationship simply reflects the stagnation of the individual's thinking pattern, which prevents the discovery of a suitable outlet for expression and satisfaction. To change a relationship we must first change our attitude and behavior toward that relationship. The relationship will inevitably change, if we are free of attachment, we will not be troubled through this inevitable transition.

We must use impermanence as an opportunity to uplift oneself and resolve tensions while remaining free of any attachment to circumstances. The clear path toward happiness is to do our best without attachment. Free of any attachment to circumstances, our mind is unobstructed like the Void. Having done our best, there is no basis for regret. Freedom from attachment is "letting go;" doing our best is the act of "taking up," or engaging. In the journey of life, we must practice letting go and taking up. We must give our best by creating wholesome thoughts, and through practice we must learn to give rise to the awareness that softens the hardened mental habits for better relationships and a better life.

Each of us, as a human being, is born into this life through the force of his or her karma, which differs in terms of attachments. Many have believed that everything simply vanishes after death, but that concept is erroneous. Unless we can untie the knots of the self-made bondage of the false I-consciousness, the cyclical pattern of birth and death will not end. The false sense of an independently existing "I" causes the accumulation of problems, concepts, experiences, judgments of right and wrong, and myriad conceptual ideas. Through this falsely conceived permanent "I," the burden is carried into everything to which we are connected.

Imagine an individual trying to carry all the consequences of a karma accumulated since time immemorial: The burden would surely be overwhelming. It is like hanging all the furniture and belongings from your relatives' and friends' homes on a little cherry tree—such a life is painful and unimaginably harsh. Lao-Tzu said, *"The reason for my great predicament is that I possess this body."* Buddha taught that having "I" is suffering. Such words of truth! Man will continually go through reincarnation unless he addresses the root of problems arising from karma. He will be confronted by the same issues in life after life, and will be stuck indefinitely where he is without any way out. Reincarnation means that we are stuck in the same grade in the school of life, having to live with the same karma again, unable to liberate ourselves from the same vexations. Man has been trapped in his own karma for so very long!

Karma follows the individual like his shadow. Wherever he goes, the mind and its karmic manifestation will also be. Therefore, it is within reason that each person must live and accept his self-made reality. Regardless of where he is, the individual carries with him a body, a personality, certain relationships and a rigid set of definitions through which he comprehends reality. Due to the limitations imposed by such definitions of reality, problems that cannot be effectively resolved by those definitions repeatedly surface in life. This is the law of karma.

Unless we attain enlightenment and actualize the Way, there is no possibility of escaping our own cyclical karma. The bondage and shadow of this cycle is the shadow of our karmic body. Only through the realization of the universal truth can liberation and freedom be attained. Only those who are truly liberated possess the capacity to uplift each relationship toward its complete fulfillment.

A person who is bound by karma is filled with vexations and problems as insurmountable as the mountains. In his world, not only does he have vexation but everyone else does as well. In his world, where everyone suffers, there is no alternative but to go through the ordeals of endless relationship dramas and difficulties. This is how great human tragedies and dramas are played out. The picture of human suffering and conflicts is that of many irregular cogs of varying sizes and shapes trying to fit together: The friction between them produces heat and light, which spread over the world. Unfortunately, this light and energy are not of wisdom or compassion; instead they are of greed, anger and delusion. A man of vexation enters a marriage only to find more vexation, and it is even more so with children. Inner sufferings and changes in the environment constantly torment him, and he is confounded as to how to resolve the inner and outer crises. Under such conditions, how can life and relationships evolve for the better?

There is no other choice than living your life—walking, standing, sitting, lying down, and interacting with people we encounter with this very body and mind. Without the body, we no longer have the karmic reflection of this present life as an individual. In fact, we are no longer ourselves, you are no longer you.

The present "you" is the condensed reflection of the entirety of your life, so to attempt escape from karma is as futile as trying to avoid your shadow under the bright sun. The present "you" is the only path; it is the only outlet for your life as a whole. Without this "you," the Collective has no ground to stand on, nor any point upon which to pivot. Outside your karma, you cannot change. Therefore, the present "you" is not merely the manifestation of the karma you have created, it is also the only pivot point by which your life can be transformed for the better. For this reason, you must take up the responsibility of your present situation and learn to transform your karma.

Whatever philosophy, spiritual tradition or method seems most appealing to you, unless you follow this universal principle, you will remain trapped in karma, unable to change it. Neither the good of living nor the good of dying will be within reach. On the other hand, if you can transform karma, the future will be in your hands.

The present moment is the best opportunity you have, so do not postpone this urgent task to yet another "tomorrow." It was once said, "Tomorrow and again tomorrow, there is always yet another tomorrow." However, ask yourself whether you will still have the opportunity and the ability to work out your karma tomorrow. The present moment already offers the turning point of your reality: Right now you can think, you can listen, see and breathe. Everything you need to make a change is already present. Seize this opportunity to make the change. Master Zhen-Jing Ke-Wen uttered the following words during the hair-shaving ceremony:

*Stunned, the hair fell like snowflakes from the blade,*
*The passage of time is merciless.*
*Strive, liberate yourself from birth and death to attain Buddhahood;*
*There is no waiting for tomorrow or the day after.*

The opportunity for practice passes by, like the moon behind a cloud. It appears ever so briefly. Impermanence is a concept that Buddhists use to remind themselves of the preciousness of time and the opportunity for practice. There is a verse that goes like this: *"Seeing others die, a fire burning in my heart. Burning not for others' sake, only that my turn will be coming."* Bodhisattva Samantabhadra admonishes all of us in the following verse: *"This day has just passed, life again is shortened. Like fish in a drying pool of water, what pleasures can be had? All beings shall make diligent efforts, saving themselves as if heads on fire."* Here we see how Buddhists use the concept of impermanence. The concept can be depressing, since it points out that impermanence is the destroyer of all existence and life is inherently instable. But seen from a different perspective, it brings freshness to every moment of life.

Impermanence never holds a grudge, nor is the hero ever troubled by his humbling past. Impermanence presents, with compassion, the opportunity for repentance in every moment. With impermanence, transformation such as *"dropping the butcher's knife, right in that moment awakening to the Buddha Nature"* becomes a possibility, but without it life is left in stagnation so that suffering remains and the Way is not attained. Because of impermanence, life is full of opportunities for transformation.

Some have believed that impermanence is nothingness, or the absence of everything, but this is a misconception. Impermanence is the principle that all phenomena of existence arise and dissolve simultaneously. Suffering is impermanent, but it is still suffering; happiness is impermanent, but it is still happiness. This is the truth as it stands.

Impermanence is not a negation of phenomena and their usefulness. Impermanence simply shows the inherent instability of phenomena. A student once asked me, "If it is indeed as the sutra stated that all phenomena are illusory and dream-like, then how should one live his life?" I said to him, "If all existence is illusion and there is nothing else, then this illusion itself becomes real. In other words, if there is nothing other than falsehood, then that falsehood becomes the truth, since it is the only thing that functions and the only thing on which one can depend."

The student then asked, "As it is stated in the *Diamond Sutra*, *'Like a dream, a phantom, a bubble floating in a stream, an illusion, like a tiny drop of dew, also like a flash of lightning. So is all conditioned existence to be seen.'* Isn't life becoming rather passive this way?"

I told him, "All existence is a dream-like existence; an existence born of grasping through false "I-consciousness;" a bubble-in-the-ocean existence; a shadow-under-the-sun existence; a momentary morning dew; and a lightning-like existence. We should perceive all phenomena as such ephemeral experiences. This sutra teaching explains the true nature of existence in order to destroy the false views in ordinary beings. It is not a negation of existence. When people take this teaching as passivity, they misunderstand its meaning." On the contrary, it is actually due to this dream-like, elusive, shadowy nature of impermanence that man is given the opportunity to change his thoughts and change his world.

Nothing in life can supplant the principle of impermanence: mind is impermanent, and form is impermanent as well. Because man has infinite possibilities for change, once he recognizes the principle of impermanence and is able to live accordingly, his life will experience a significant improvement. We cannot attain true freedom without living our life according to the principle of impermanence.

All suffering comes from the individual, who is imprisoned by his attempts to act against the principle of impermanence. The nature of self-attachment, stubborn thinking, habitual tendencies, prejudice, opinions, personalities, subjective beliefs and so forth is in conflict with the principle of impermanence. Self-centered thinking and behavior patterns should be replaced with a deep conviction in the universal principle, and new ways of thinking should be cultivated. Over time, this practice will yield a great benefit. Once the cultivation has reached its full maturity so that all attachments have been eradicated, the individual will experience the indescribable state of Oneness with the truth. This is Zen's so-called training and cultivation in the Essence of the Mind.

The nature of the Mind consists of primordial awareness, primordial emptiness and primordial liberation. Phenomena go through transformations from the substrate of the Mind without any obstruction, due to the Mind's primordially liberated characteristic. Just as the sun, the moon, the celestial constellations and the myriad phenomena of earth are changing, coming and going in the Void, the Void can manifest impermanence but is neither born nor destroyed. The essence of the mind is primordial awareness, primordial emptiness and primordial liberation, manifesting impermanence through phenomena in the void; through different phenomena, the innate impermanence of the Mind becomes manifest. This is the Mind's primordial liberation.

Because the Mind is emptiness, it is liberated; because it is impermanent, it is liberated. Since the Mind is selfless and formless, and since form is not form in itself, the form is liberated. In the phenomenon, the Mind is selfless, and this is the cause of its primordial liberation. If we can realize this principle and act accordingly, we will experience what Zen Master Da-Hui described in the following: "*When the bottom of the bucket falls, the great earth opens its vastness. Where the root of Life terminates, the lake is purified. Like a flake of snow fallen on a red-hot stove, it spreads among men as the nightly illumination.*"

## Empty Mind, Vast Cosmos

The occupied mind perceives the universe as something narrow, as if it has contracted. But the mind that is clear and free of preoccupation, sees the universe as vast and wide. An open mind can accept new concepts and adapt to situations and challenges. The ancients said, "*The mind turns with situation, but this turning point is most profound and subtle; going with the flow while recognizing the essence, there is neither excitement nor depression.*" A flexible, pliable state of mind is receptive to new ideas and is able to receive benefit from them. This is just like Lao-Tzu's famous teaching that the *ultimate goodness is to be like water.*

A flexible, pliable mind is free in every moment of thought creation, unburdened by various factors. Such a mind can easily change its mode of thinking without holding onto stale conclusions and poor habits. It is free of self-attachment and able to do its best when confronting any situation. The mind in this state can deal with reality on its own terms, handling reality as it is.

A pliable, adaptable mind is one in which deluded thoughts have been withdrawn. Only a mind that is free of delusion can enjoy true freedom and self-mastery. A mind that is burdened with attachment to past experiences only makes mistakes in its perception of reality, and suffers from poor judgment and misguided handling of situations in life. A burdened mind cannot see reality as reality, nor can such a mind deal with reality as it is. A burdened mind is the obstacle to man's learning and spiritual development.

A well-known scholar of Japan's Meiji period paid a visit to a Nanyin Zen master in order to discuss Zen. The master politely showed the visitor to his seat and began to pour tea. The master slowly poured the tea into a cup until it spilled over the table and onto the floor. Seeing no sign that the master intended to stop, he cried out, "Master! The tea has spilled over, the cup cannot hold any more. Please stop!" The Nanyin master then replied very peacefully, *"Like this tea cup, your mind is already filled with ideas, and there is no room for learning anything new. If you do not empty the cup that is yourself, how can I tell you about Zen?"*

You may react to this story by saying, "I've heard this before," or "Even a three-year-old knows this," or "This is too simple," or "The point is about humility." Yes, you may have indeed heard this story, but the mind that responds this way is still filled with judgments. A three-year-old may have learned about this, but that does not mean an adult can actually accomplish it. The story is truly simple, but in this moment your mind might be too occupied with opinions and commentaries to receive the teaching. Lastly, if you say the story is about humility, the attitude with which the comment is made could be quite arrogant. When your immediate response to the story is that we should have a mind as calm as still water, that is true humility. The selfless mind is the most humble of all.

Pride gives an individual the illusion of wisdom: He acts as if he knows everything, and therefore he tends to be argumentative with others. In reality, such a person is under the control of self-centered I-consciousness. Those with strong I-consciousness tend to behave with exuberant confidence and are unreceptive to suggestions by others. The unconscious display of self-importance and a know-it-all attitude are signs of pride and self-attachment. Such an individual would find learning impossible and the prospect of making real change very slim. His life is stuck in confusion and ignorance, like a beggar claiming to be a king.

New ideas can only enter an open mind. A mind occupied with preconceived notions loses opportunities for learning; the saying, "*Humility brings benefit, pride invites harm, the empty heart of bamboo is my teacher*" means just this. Life's problems come in all forms, but most people do not realize there is only one real problem, which is that of attachment to the false I-consciousness and its tendency to grasp phenomena in order to feel secure.

Essentially, a life built on self-attachment will see the same problems repeated over and over again in various forms to the point where the individual wonders, "Where did all these problems come from!?" However, there is just one fundamental problem:

the grasping of phenomena by the I-consciousness. While many problems can occur in a life, all problems belong to he who lives it. Like the viruses that cannot yet be eradicated by medical science, the problem may be transformed into a new kind of virus depending on the changes in conditions. Regardless of the form, its harmful nature remains.

As you read this book, do not filter these concepts through your past experiences. There is a Zen saying, "*To intend is already off-base; to think misses the truth.*" In other words, open your mind completely to the present moment. The past is no longer the reality, but the reality is instead this present moment. Only the manifestation in the present moment is tangible.

The Mind gives rise to all, manifests all and contains all. Zen Master Lin-Ji said: "*The Mind-Dharma is formless, completely pervades the ten directions—in the eyes it becomes the seeing, in the ears it becomes the hearing, in the nose the smelling, in the mouth the speaking, in the hands the grasping, in the feet the running; originally one essence, but expressed as the six contacts between sense and objects. This one Mind is emptiness, and all are liberated where they are. Now we seek intimacy with the true hearer of dharma: the formless, shapeless, rootless, baseless, non-abiding, alive and energetic.*" The functioning of the Mind is directly manifested as phenomena; each action, and every word spoken, results from the Mind's functioning. From the point of functioning in this present moment, extending to the entire universe, the existence of the entire dharma realm unfolds in the Mind.

Man's unconscious mental activity sets the course of his life. With the Mind, he generates thoughts and creates karma, and with the same Mind he can redirect his thoughts and change his karma. When the modality of mental functioning changes, the Mind and the phenomena it encompasses will also change. This is the Mind-Dharma. Understand the Mind and the Mind-Dharma, and every problem can be resolved.

The mind is pliable and alive when thoughts can change easily. When the mind is pliable and lively, it is easier to change the thought. The degree of mental flexibility and the ability to change thoughts go hand in hand. This is similar to the idea that the more we exercise the brain, the sharper it gets. So, one way to cultivate the ability to change thoughts is to practice not letting the mind become occupied with stubborn ones. With this mental skill, we find abundant opportunities in everyday life, and we will be surrounded by favorable conditions. Moreover, the broad range of thinking developed by this practice allows us to acquire new concepts.

The individual who confronts an unsatisfactory outcome in life should try to face the reality. He should practice recognizing the opportunity within the situation and stop the pattern of complaining. Complaint is a thought created in reaction to an undesirable phenomenon, and as such it becomes inseparable from the undesired phenomenon. To complain will only exacerbate the situation instead of improving it. In order to redirect the manner in which reality unfolds, we should create a different pattern of mind functioning within the situation's reality.

The pattern of mind functioning is the cause of a problem, and the thought that arises from this pattern is the result. If the obstinate pattern of mind functioning is changed, the individual will improve his ability to change his thoughts as well as the direction of his life. Therefore, we should first be certain of the kind of life we want to create and then apply this principle of the Mind's functioning in our life in a very practical manner, in accordance with the principle of causality. When a problem occurs, we should find a new path of opportunity so that the karma and result we experience in such a situation will gradually change. Since we find ourselves in a life characterized by a mixture of the desirable and the undesirable—of positive and negative situations—we must change our thoughts, or we will face limitations wherever we go. And we will suffer accordingly.

## A World of Opinions

Unless the individual eradicates the I-consciousness, the problems he encounters during this lifetime will become embedded in his I-consciousness, awaiting the maturation of appropriate conditions and contacts with certain phenomena so that their manifestations will be triggered. Like a seed that holds the potential of a fully grown tree and all its attributes, the seed will mature given the proper soil conditions, sunlight, moisture and a sufficiency of time. The existing pattern of mind functioning, concept and belief within an individual's mind establishes the basis for the maturation of his future karma.

Problems are not created by singular instances of thought. Instead, it is the accumulated result of repeatedly grasping phenomena and accumulating reactions as an unconscious mode of mind functioning. Just as Rome was not built in a day, no major problem or issue can appear unless it is preceded by the long, unconscious incubation of a certain pattern of functioning. Despite this fact, however, man continues to seek the instant elimination of problems.

Each occurrence of unconscious thought creation reinforces the thought and its power to dominate the individual, reducing the degree of freedom in the mind. The human mind becomes increasingly rigid as it solidifies certain personality traits and their inherent problems. This path eventually leads to a stubborn inner mental environment and a paralyzed outer situation.

Delusion hides reality and traps the individual within his predicaments. In such a condition, the individual tends to attribute his issues to other people or situations, blaming others due to his own lack of effort. A mind that is occupied by attachment has no room left for the truth, and it uses various emotions to reject undesirable realities. Emotion is not the root cause of a problem but is only the external sign of a problem whose source is deeper. The real cause of a problem is the self-attachment deep within the mind. The unconscious interaction between a pattern of mind functioning and its environment is the key factor that worsens the problem. Therefore, any antidote must be administered directly to the attachment, the unconscious functioning pattern deep in the mind.

The body and emotion are similar, in that they are the outer reflections of inner attachment as expressed through unconscious mind functioning. They are the results, not the causes; they are therefore transitory. Of course, unpleasant results are disturbing to life and must be handled properly. For example, if we become ill then the symptoms should be treated in order to minimize their impact on our quality of life. However, the key is to identify the cause of the illness and apply the remedy directly in order to effect a permanent cure.

Life's problems are much like the physical symptoms of illness. They require adjustments, time and energy in order to be handled properly. However, the problems in our present life situation are merely outer manifestations, while the root of these problems is the accumulation of attachment over countless lifetimes. On the spiritual level, this is the fundamental problem that requires a resolution.

It is said that to defeat the bandits, first capture their leader. We should definitely manage the surface symptoms well, but more importantly our effort should be invested in effecting a cure at the root cause of the illness. Similarly, we should deal with the problems in this lifetime, but the more important task is to address the deeper cause of the present and future suffering. If we merely dance with the superficial, emotional display of a problem, we cannot see the real cause. Regardless of how much effort we commit, it will only result in the waste of a life spent dancing with deluded thoughts.

We have no choice other than to skillfully use the conditions available in our present life to redirect our way of thinking. Others cannot do it for us, nor are they responsible, since only the one who has tied the bell around the lion's neck can untie it. It is not the point whether or not we like an existing problem; what really matters is the fact that the problem is already part of our life. It is difficult to truly face our thoughts.

In fact, if every thought an individual has could take on a physical form, it would probably look like a monstrous creature, frightening even to himself. Our minds have become like sewage filled with the stench of greed, hatred and delusion, as well as the urges for killing, stealing and sensual desire. Still, we have no choice but to face this reality, since to do otherwise is to remain in this toxic mental environment. If we are unwilling to face the harsh truth of life, we cannot use the challenges and problems we encounter to develop the right view. Instead, we will live with considerable dissatisfaction and denial. To flow with habitual tendencies perpetuates future suffering, but the spiritual practice of self-transformation is the sensible path. The right course is to correct our thinking and continue learning throughout life.

Most people are open to learning new concepts and knowledge during their formative years in school. After graduation, however, they enter the big bucket of mixed dye that is society, whereupon they soak up all kinds of habitual tendencies as problems begin to emerge in daily life. Nonetheless, such a person will not hesitate to give others advice on how to live a good life, like the blind leading the blind.

We also find spiritual practitioners who have created great amounts of vexation due to their lack of the right view. They urge friends and relatives to practice in the same way they do, like a person jumping into a pit of fire and dragging a few others with him. In various ways, false views have been passed from one person to another, as explained in the following: "*The ignorant teaches the ignorant, and both remain ignorant. The teachers descend to Hell, and the students push their way in, too.*"

There is a story in the Buddhist scripture about the blind and the elephant. One day a group of blind men who had never seen an elephant before tried to find out what an elephant was like. Each person, after touching the elephant, described what he thought to the group. The first person touched the elephant's tail, so he told the group: "The elephant is like a broom." The second person touched the elephant's feet and said, "The elephant is like a big, tall stool." The third person touched the nose and said, "No, the elephant is like a big water pipe." Finally they got together and discussed the elephant's appearance, and they concluded that the elephant was something between a broom, a stool and a water pipe.

Clearly, none of their perceptions were the truth because their definitions of the truth all differed. Truth is the truth, however, so it must be clear and simple. The manifestation of truth is the reality; it is the result we experience. Based on the result, we can deduce the cause and correct it so that the result will change for the better. Reality is the maturation of phenomenon in the coming together of various factors and conditions: This is the Buddhist concept of dependent origination. The mere existence of reality is sufficient to demonstrate the presence of underlying factors and conditions in the required proportions.

Reality does not require our explanation, nor is our explanation ever the reality. If we hold onto our own definition of reality, how can reality ever be seen? We must reflect and ask ourselves why we have a certain definition and perspective about things so we can penetrate to the source of problems.

In each moment, an individual's thought demonstrates the

rigidity of his mind, because whatever is seen, heard and thought of can never be separated from his inner definition of reality. Therefore, instead of saying that we see or hear reality, it is more accurate to say that we are seeing and hearing our own definition of reality, created by our inner attachments and prejudices.

For example, a person will speak the language of his childhood and become habituated to a certain tradition. Even after adulthood and exposure to the outside world, his concepts, accent and life experiences will still be largely shaped by his background. Because of this conditioning, people from diverse backgrounds always have their own opinions, and inevitably this world is one of duality.

## To Purify the Senses Is the Way

Many practitioners in the history of Buddhism have fasted as a method of practice, sometimes going seven days or more without anything other than water. On one hand, the purpose of such training is to reduce greed; on the other hand, its purpose is to strengthen and stabilize the mind under stressful conditions. In the face of hunger, anger or depression, a practitioner should be aware of his emotions through the concentrated application of mindful awareness. If he is able to accomplish this, then his habitually negative reactions and thoughts can be tamed. For the sake of training himself to release negative thoughts, the practitioner will sometimes deliberately enter a problematical situation.

Zen describes the unenlightened mind as a wild ox: If not controlled, the ox can hurt people and trample the crops. Similarly, if a person cannot gain mastery over his own mind by controlling his thoughts and emotions, he will be led into the abyss of inner conflict.

Many Zen students have told me, "I want to stop the wandering thoughts, but I just cannot control myself." Others have asked me, "If I cannot control anger, how can I change my life?" If you really cannot help yourself, then how can I help you? In that case, you have no choice but to enjoy your problems! Sometimes that would be my response to these questions, because it is the truth, or, in other words, their truth and reality. It has been said that "God helps those who help themselves." If you can open a new door in your life, new experiences will enter.

Keep the mind open and flexible in every moment. If you cannot face life's reality but instead remain in a state of delusion, true freedom will not be yours. There is no free lunch under the sun, since each measure of effort brings its own reward. A Zen poem goes like this: "*Sprouts in hand I plant them in the soil; looking down I see the reflection of sky in the water. Purifying the six senses is the Way, stepping back is really moving forward.*"

We are the sole cultivators of our own lives, so only by withdrawing from the proliferation of all the homeless, wandering thoughts can we master our own lives. It has been said: "*Life's trials and tribulations are many, created by oneself and experienced by oneself; why is there trouble being tolerant and receptive?*" If we can live with this understanding, life will be vast as the sky and wide as the earth; the dust of right and wrong shall vanish with a smile. There is no place where we cannot settle our body in peace. Life is truly grand.

The Sixth Patriarch of Zen taught his disciples: "*Just use this Mind, directly actualize Buddhahood.*" My conviction regarding this principle has lead me to engage in spiritual practice. Before I entered the monastic life, I was interviewed by a journalist who asked me, "Once you have taken the monastic vow, what is it that you want to accomplish?" I replied, "Wherever I go, I shall commit my best effort to transforming that place into a Pureland." The journalist was aghast upon hearing this, "But how could you accomplish that? You are not the Buddha!"

I said to him, "Perhaps right now I cannot establish a Pureland, but as long as I continue to make the effort, one day my aspiration will come true and I shall attain Buddhahood." The goal of liberation and freedom is not far, and with a mind that is flexible and lively there is always room to arouse mindful awareness. As long as our concept and understanding are correct, no matter how far away the destination might be, arrival is assured.

Everything in life changes from one moment to the next. If we recognize this impermanence and live with it, we will be able to change our thoughts and find fresh opportunities in everything. Remember, each thought affects our body, our relationships and our life, so we should commit our greatest effort to treating everyone around us with loving-kindness, compassion and equanimity. Cultivate now while there is a chance, and seize these precious moments to accomplish our great awakening.

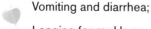

> Plagued by indigestion,
> Vomiting and diarrhea;
> Longing for my Home,
> Difficult to appreciate the bright Moon tonight.

# 7  SERENE MIND IN THE JADE JUG

Hush, hush, make not a sound,

Joshu is in my dream;

The Sixth Patriarch's bowl just tamed the dragons,

Awakened, the day is bright outside my window.

Zen discourses may seem aloof and somewhat high-brow, but at their foundation is the gut-wrenching, unrelenting process of subduing the untamed mind. It is not easy to penetrate to the essence of the Mind, but the freedom and perfect ease of the ancient sages came from their unyielding effort to destroy attachments. Master Huang-Bo once said:

*Extrication from the fatigue of duality is no ordinary matter,*
*Hold on tight to the beginning of the rope and give your best,*
*Without experiencing that bone-piercing chill,*
*How could you smell the fragrant plum?*

Without the right view, correct guidance and effort, spiritual attainment will be difficult.

Today's practitioners tend to develop a sense of pride once they gain some minor understanding from reading Zen koans or the recorded dialogues of enlightened sages. The masters of Zen have referred to such people as "those who become sickly and dripping wet under examination." In a hectic society, people's minds are unstable and filled with material desires, negative emotions and tension. Through meditation one can train the mind, calm the emotions and eliminate the chaotic mental state. The practice of meditation has been around for thousands of years, and it is very effective in eliminating habitual tendencies and attachments so that the practitioner may regain mastery of his mind and thoughts. Because it is so worthwhile, seated meditation is a key method in Zen training; it is a practice worth cultivating, life after life.

Besides improving one's mastery of mental activities, the ultimate goal of Zen training is enlightenment, the maturation of wisdom, and the awakening of our self and others until we attain the complete, perfect Buddhahood. There is no phenomenon outside the Mind, nor is there Mind outside phenomena. When we attain the realization of the Way, we experience the Pure Mind and are able to function from its most essential basis.

The Mind manifests all forms, and all forms are inseparable from the Mind. Therefore, to attain realization we must first eliminate our false sense of independent selfhood and attachment to habitual tendencies. This is the initial step in Zen training. Before we are able to illuminate the essence and function of the Pure Mind, our mind functions unconsciously.

Only through the complete destruction of the false selfhood can the mind enter a state of purity, clarity and complete awakening, illuminating all Mind functioning and manifestations to experience a selfless essence as vast as the Great Void, to encompass myriad phenomena without confusion. In this way, the individual not only enjoys greater peace and fulfillment, but he also develops a personal conviction that nirvana and complete liberation are not fictitious, nonexistent abstractions. They are the truth, directly achievable by everyone.

## Only Because One Is in the Mountain

Seated meditation is the most effective method of purifying and calming the mind. Only the cessation of deluded thoughts can reveal the Mind's essential nature. The essence of Mind is emptiness, awareness and luminosity. The True Mind, Pure Mind, Buddha Mind, Bodhi, the Other Shore and the Pureland are all terms describing the Mind that is free from the defilements of the false self, delusion, confusion, definitions and judgments. They are the names that represent the manifestation of the Mind's original nature. The True Mind is selfless, and only through selflessness can the truth be expressed without distortion.

Zen describes three stages in the progression of a practitioner's training. The first of these is described as *"seeing the mountain as mountain, seeing the water as water—with ignorance of the Mind's function and essence."* The second stage is *"seeing the mountain not as mountain; seeing the water not as water—begin the process of purification."* The final stage is *"seeing the mountain again as mountain, seeing the water again as water—union of the Mind's function and essence."*

Man's original nature unconsciously creates a false "I-consciousness" through which he repeatedly arouses similar thoughts until an inflexible mental and behavioral pattern is developed. This is the so-called self-attachment. The original Pure Mind is emptiness and selflessness. Due to ignorance, the distinctions of so-called inner and outer realities are created. The individual identifies with only a fraction of the his Mind's creation, an amalgam of his physical body and independent consciousness, his true self and his inner reality.

The Pure Mind defiled by self-attachment gives rise to delusion, judgment and definitions that unconsciously distort the truth. But different modes of mind functioning produce different mental definitions of phenomena. For example, when a believer is in the presence of a Buddha statue, he applies a mental definition of reverence to the process of perceiving the statue. This perception results in the behavior of prostration, even though the Buddha statue is only materialistic. As human beings, we do not recognize the truth in their perception. Instead, we apply definitions that substitute for the truth. This concept is captured in the Zen saying, *"Anything that is said lacks real meaning."*

The Mind and truth can only be recognized through direct experience. When a human being defines everything so that nothing can transcend his definitions, his life is locked inside the world as he defines it. This reality is very narrow with respect to the mind's capacity. Narrow-mindedness causes strong opinions and beliefs that reject others, makes relationships difficult and exaggerates situations. For example, if a person sits on a chair he is unaccustomed to, he may think, "This chair is very uncomfortable, and I don't like it. I really like my chair." Habitual judgments block a person's capacity to adapt to people, situations and the environment.

Prejudice and deluded judgments can conceal the real problem, making it difficult for the individual to recognize and admit his shortcomings. Failing to see the root of his problem, the individual enters a holding pattern of isolated living, paralyzed within the prison of self-constructed definition. For that reason, the dedicated Zen student focuses on breaking the bondage imposed by his definition of reality; he commits his entire life to destroying attachment and attaining enlightenment.

It is said that before Zen training the individual "sees the mountain as mountain, the water as water." Because he tries to understand reality through his attachment, nothing is able to transcend his definition of reality. Moreover, because at this stage no one can transcend his definition, the perception of mountain can only be based on a preconceived notion. Such preconceived notions create a false reality. When the individual perceives phenomenon, he actually apprehends only the thought. The thought is only part of the totality of the Mind's functioning; it is not the truth.

In addition to using these definitions to react to reality, the deluded individual also uses them to interpret reality. As in a home-made movie, the individual writes the script, directs the performance and is the actor. His life is a one-man show that comprises nothing more than the monologue of the sole character in the story, the self. The poet Xu Dong-Po once wrote: "*Looking across, it is a ridge, looking from the side, it becomes a peak. Near, far, high, and low, appearances are each distinct. One sees not the true face of Mt. Lu, only because he is in the mountain.*" Any interpretation arrived at through an individual's interpretation of reality are only attachment. The first stage of Zen training teaches that the practitioner "sees the mountain as mountain, the water as water" through his own definition—this is not yet the reality.

## Definition of Reality Is the Framework of Life

Man unconsciously builds his prison, the framework of his definition of reality. In the process he molds his originally limitless, formless and free mind into a collection of independent, oddly shaped fragments. Before enlightenment, man sees his definition instead of the truth; after Zen training, he begins the process of breaking down attachments in order to become free from his misconception of reality. In other words, he starts to cast doubt on his view of things. At this stage he "sees the mountain not as mountain, water not as water."

In casting doubt on his own beliefs, man eventually recognizes that these definitions are unable to reflect the truth. In this stage of the training, due to the negation of his old definitions of self and reality, the mountain is no longer seen as mountain, and water is no longer seen as water. Here, the Zen practitioner gains conviction in the necessity of self-inquiry to challenge his usual expectation and view of the world. If he remains ignorant of how he creates his definitions and reacts to them, he will continue to take his own views and understandings as the truth.

The purpose of this book is to show you how man has applied his definitions to the truth. If you believe that you understand the idea I am conveying, you are reacting habitually to your own definitions. If your interpretation of spiritual teachings cannot correctly reflect the truth, you only reflect my conception of that teaching. The Buddha once told his students that if everyone in the world thinks what he or she believes is correct, then the world will not have truth. It is a universal truth that "*everyone believes in what he believes.*"

Many practitioners have studied the scriptures and practiced different methods. Until their subjective beliefs and views of reality are eliminated, they cannot attain enlightenment. The layman Pong wrote a poem that goes like this: "*Reading without understanding, the mind of many opinions is worse off than blindness. Grasping the written words, many plots of land are occupied. But without cultivating the mind— weeds grown everywhere—from where could any grains grow?*" Moreover, the *Complete Awakening Sutra* says, "*To speculate regarding Complete Awakening within samsara, the nature of Complete Awakening becomes transitory. To desire freedom from samsara in this way is falsehood.*" To truly engage in the training of Mind-Dharma, we must relinquish preconceived prejudice. Seated meditation is very effective in freeing the mind from habitual thoughts.

In meditation, wandering thoughts quickly emerge, clearly evidencing the practitioner's lack of mastery over the mind. When the mind is out of control, habitual thinking manifests without awareness, and the presence of such thinking demonstrates that the practitioner has not yet become the master of his own mind. Instead, he continues to live unconsciously, marching blindly toward an unknown future. Without awareness, the mind gives rise to thoughts, definitions and judgments in response to phenomena, functioning in a manner similar to that of a sleepwalker. To such a person, the day is a dream and the night is also a dream; life itself is a dream. Master Yong-Jia once said, "*Clearly the six realms exist in our dream, empty is the universe after awakening.*" In the hour of awakening, we realize that life is just a dream.

Countless unconscious thoughts have been born in our present lifetime. The activity of the I-consciousness gives habitual tendencies the strength to generate wandering thoughts of delusion. These thoughts fly through the mental landscape without our awareness of where they come from or where they will go. Wandering thoughts come from the self-attachment that resides in the subconscious level of the mind, the unconscious aspect of the mind in which self-attachment is very strong. Specifically, the depth of the subconscious activities depends on the strength of self-attachment: Stronger thoughts of attachment deepen the subconscious mind, but when the subconscious mind functions, it strengthens the self-attachment. Attachment and subconscious functioning reinforce one another in a downward spiral that allows prejudice and deluded judgments to seize control of life.

Consider the example of a buffet restaurant, where a great variety of foods are always available. Through the influence of the subconscious mind people tend to focus their attention on a few dishes that they either like or dislike the most, as if the other dishes do not exist. After the meal, if you ask someone to recall all the choices that were available, he will preferentially remember the foods associated with his strong attachments. His unconscious patterns of mind functioning filter and distort the truth. These habitual tendencies act as filters that prevent a person from seeing the truth that is present in his or her life.

Myriad unconscious thoughts fill the mind in daily life. When the individual settles his mind in meditation by closing his eyes in silence, his deluded and wandering thoughts will gradually become pacified. At this point, he is able to observe the deeper level of the subconscious mind and bring its content into the light of awareness, elevating the unconscious to the level of the conscious awareness. In other words, as wandering thoughts fade, the relative strength of awareness increases and presents the practitioner with opportunities to recognize and dissolve the inertia of unconscious mental habits. This is the process of de-conditioning from mental habits and deluded tendencies.

One must first see the thief before the thief can be caught. Similarly, any method of practice must serve to transform the unconscious into the conscious in order to dissolve the construct of the false "I." Without this transformation, any effort will be fruitless. Whether it is the surface or the deeper levels of the I-consciousness, ultimately the unconscious tendencies must be eradicated to reveal the true nature of the Mind. If the practitioner cannot develop a higher degree of relative awareness, even years of meditation will not produce tangible results. In Zen, this is described as *"the deluded world of make-believe in the ghostly, dark mountain cave of ignorance."*

Without developing inner illumination, a practitioner's awareness becomes dull, and he is unable to recognize his own delusion. Instead, he mistakes the state of mental lethargy—the dullness of awareness—as mental purity and tranquility. This is a false view of practice, the result of which is likened to soaking a stone in cold water: nothing can be accomplished. It is very important for all practitioners to understand this concept.

## Thought Is the Mind's Servant

Before we break attachments and attain enlightenment, every instance of mind functioning arises through the I-consciousness. Breaking attachments is the destruction of the unconscious mode of mind functioning. When we think and act according to our habitual tendencies, our thinking goes on autopilot in a fixed direction, and in the process we lose all initiative.

It has been said that habit is man's second nature, by which he instinctively responds to situations without conscious reason. People, when asked why they respond in certain ways, will often answer, "I don't know." However, amid the silence of seated meditation the mind quiets down, and at this point it becomes easier to recognize the wandering thoughts that arise from the deeper levels of the I-consciousness. Through this process, we are able to obtain insight into the nature of wandering thoughts and see that they are groundless.

Wandering thoughts have no basis in reality; otherwise, it would be impossible to sever them from the mind. Because wandering thoughts lack a truly substantial existence, to practice with the intent of cutting off wandering thoughts is actually to place one kind of falsehood atop another. If delusion has no basis in the truth, why bother cutting it off? The concept of cutting off wandering thought is simply an expedient way of expressing the objective. Simply stop following up on thought movements—do not continue the generation of deluded thought—and thoughts will dissipate like fallen ash on the ground. They will simply cease.

Wandering thoughts are produced through I-consciousness, as

the functioning of ignorance. Ignorance, when traced to its source, is simply the unconscious state of mind created by self-attachment. Self-attachment is the grasping of phenomena and the identification of a pattern of unconscious functioning as the self. Attachment, due to its nature, functions by chasing after phenomena, setting the individual adrift from the flow of his karma. This can be likened to monkeys in the forest constantly jumping from one branch to the next without a moment's rest.

A great reward results from the practice of meditation. It is the realization of the statement, "*Grasp the mind with the mind, create illusion out of that which is not illusion.*" Meditation serves to reveal the nearly imperceptible but subtly powerful habits of the I-consciousness, or the so-called subconscious mind, and lifts them into conscious awareness. Given the heightened level of relative awareness developed during meditation, the unconscious habits can be recognized and deconstructed. Continuing further with the practice, we understand how we actually give power to the stream of wandering thoughts, allowing them to control his life and thereby create a future of ignorance.

A person who becomes angry and reacts habitually is giving strength to that reaction, and each subsequent instance of anger further reinforces the reaction. This habit will ultimately lead the individual toward such a situation in which he will have no choice but to use anger again as his only response. Therefore, if he unconsciously employs certain habitual thoughts, by forming and following these habitual patterns of thought creation he will carve a highway of such thoughts. The course of that highway will consist of, and lead to, repetitive thinking and reactions.

Emotion is the accumulation of a series of similar thoughts. We can compare this to the concept of aggregate in the *Four Noble Truths*, namely *suffering*, *aggregate* (cause of suffering), *cessation* and the *path leading to cessation*. All emotions and habits result from the aggregation of similar thoughts, which are of course habitual. Emotion is a function of the aggregation centered around "self," in which the sustained creation of forceful thoughts forms afflictive emotions. Unless we can gain mastery over our own mind, emotional reactions will overwhelm our awareness. However, if we are able to master our thoughts by disengaging the repetitive tendency toward unconscious thoughts, we will achieve control over our emotions and give rise to mind functioning with detachment and conscious control. We will therefore reach the state of complete, unobtrusive natural ease.

Thoughts and emotions are the tools we use to cultivate our life; the tools for managing and responding to people, situations and our environment. As tools, they should be subservient to us instead of behaving as our master. Before we can take rein of our mind functioning, we will frequently suffer at the hands of afflictive emotions, which will become obstacles that render futile any response to a situation. Without recognizing this, life's direction and quality will be dictated by the emotions. If we use emotions that have no benefit in terms of a given situation, we repeat the same flawed decision-making process.

Because all problems, burdens and obstacles stem from negative mental habits, we must improve our situation by adopting new, more effective modes of response. The first, most important step is to regularly practice meditation in order to establish mental calm and focus, thereby relaxing the phenomena-grasping tendency so as to illuminate and dissolve destructive habits. Through meditation, we gradually realize the true master to be the Mind, and at this point thought becomes its servant. Thoughts, emotions, behaviors and reactions are all produced by the Mind. They are the servants— the tools—but only the Mind is the master. Suffering is inevitable if the roles of master and servant are reversed, because that which is false is accepted as truth.

## Meditation, the Powerful Tool of Thought Transformation

The famed poet Su Dong Po, of the Sung dynasty, composed the following verse to express his attainment: *"Prostrate to the heaven among the heavens, light of a single hair strand illuminates the universe. Imperturbable by the eight worldly winds, seated firmly upon the golden purple lotus."* The *eight worldly winds* are praise, censure, disgrace, honor, prosperity, decline, suffering and pleasure; these are the eight things that most occupy the mind of an ordinary individual. When the mind is hooked by the phenomenon, it grasps it then becomes unstable, like the dust blown back and forth on the breeze. These eight winds restrict and disturb the mind, causing mental laxity and weakened focus.

Su Dong Po was proud of his practice as well as this poem, so he decided to send it to his good friend across the river, Zen Master Foyin, so that he could enjoy it, too. After reading the poem,

Master Foyin smiled and commented on the back of the letter (in two Chinese words) "Fart!" and dispatched his attendant to take the poem back across the river. After reading the comment, Su Dong Po became irate and boarded a boat immediately, intending to argue with the Zen master face to face. When they finally met, Master Foyin said to him, "I thought you could not be perturbed by the eight winds, but now apparently two words have already blown you all the way across the river!"

It is not easy for most people to understand and accept the idea that the Mind is the source of life and that all thoughts are created by the Mind, but it is even more difficult for a beginning student to accept the concept that all problems are of his own making. However, these are universal truths. As the Mind functions the phenomenon is born: This is among the fundamental tenets of Zen, and it is the origin of the principle of cause and effect. Such ideas are not easy to accept because they challenge man's self-centered habits and engender fear of acceptance, or the anxiety of not knowing how to face such a truth.

Because self-attachment is not willing to face the truth, the mind remains trapped in the I-consciousness and loses its balance as it continues to protect the "self." Furthermore, faith that our own mind already completely encompasses all in its essence is lost, and we are unable to stop the pursuit of selfhood by which we habitually grasp at external phenomena. Ironically, the Mind does possess and encompass all that is, just as the ancients said: "*Within each man is a mind, within each mind a cosmos; know the ancient Buddha what is seated within, and seek not the universe outside the Mind.*"

The mind gives rise to habitual thoughts, and these thoughts define the scope of self-attachment. It is self-attachment to grasp the habitual thoughts as "I," and the range of activity of self-attachment is defined by the range of activity of habitual thoughts. The range of thoughts cannot override the habits from which they are generated. Habitual thoughts often occupy and surround the mind. The instant they emerge, the mind seizes one from among many thoughts and identifies with that thought as *mine*, as *what "I" think*. In that instant, the "I" is nothing more than that thought, and that thought defines "I" in the moment.

The mind, as one engages in meditation practice, will continue to generate many thoughts, but without grasping them and instead concentrating only on the method, these various thoughts—each of which can potentially be perceived as what the "I" thinks—are now nothing but wandering thoughts. When the mind identifies with a thought, it becomes the "I," but when the mind refrains from identifying with the thoughts they become so-called "wandering thoughts." During meditation, wandering thoughts will appear and disturb the clarity of the mind. It is essential not to follow these mental movements but to continue to focus exclusively on the method of meditation. When there is no wandering, do not grasp such a state of mind as emptiness. Do not follow up on one thought movement with another, nor seize the absence of thought as emptiness. Remain in a state of equanimity and these thoughts, due to their nature, will eventually cease.

In a practitioner with superior aptitude, the mind can become intimate with the authentic self-nature. Otherwise, one should at least be resolutely focused upon the method of cultivation: Do not actively seek emptiness but instead let it come on its own accord, so that the wandering thoughts will arise and self-liberate while the primordial nature of the Mind remains. In response to the poet Bai, Zen Master Daolin composed this verse: "*Traceless in coming and going, Undistinguishable in coming and going; why be concerned with worldly affairs? This fleeting life is just a dream.*" Through the intentional cultivation of thoughts that resonate with practice without engaging wandering thoughts, we can break free from our habitually unconscious tendencies.

Meditation is the reversal of the process that establishes our habitual tendencies; consequently, the establishment of habitual tendencies is due to the repetition of similar thoughts. If we are able to refrain from following these thoughts, thus stopping the process of creating and building them up, the reversal of the formation process begins to free us from the habit. The mind will then return to its original, pure ground. Because delusion arises from the mind, the original purity of the Mind can be recovered by removing the delusion. Apply the ways of the enemy against the enemy. Meditation is a very effective method of dissolving habitual tendencies. Through focused meditation, the practitioner continually disengages from wandering thought. These thoughts, when ignored, will gradually be deprived of their strength.

Practitioners are occasionally surprised to notice wandering thoughts and will ask, "Why do I have so many wandering thoughts during meditation?" The fact is that meditation does not create more wandering thoughts. However, due to the lack of gross phenomena for the mind to grasp, the outward-driven phenomena-seeking tendency, which is still active, will be manifested in the form of chaotic, wandering thoughts.

The emergence of thoughts despite the absence of phenomena on which they normally depend during meditation is referred to as wandering, or scattered, thought. During meditation, the mind cannot grasp external phenomena, so it becomes more aware of previously unknown activities in the deeper level of the I-consciousness. This is the reason that the sustained practice of meditation will cultivate and deepen awareness, and gradually reduce wandering thoughts. For example, when we want to distance ourselves from certain friends or relationships, we simply reduce the occasions and time we spend with them until eventually they disappear from our lives. We should handle wandering thoughts in much the same way. By gradually withdrawing the habit of following up on wandering thoughts, they will eventually disappear due to a lack of attention.

Wandering thoughts are like undesirable acquaintances: Ignore them when they call you and instead focus on practicing the meditation method. Do not allow wandering thoughts to occupy your attention, because doing so makes them stronger. Do not lose concentration by becoming attracted to the illusory phenomena they produce. Each time your attention follows the wandering thoughts instead of the method of practice, you strengthen the wandering thoughts. Mental concentration is the means by which meditation calms the mind. The ability to master and direct our thought is cultivated through focused meditative practice, which enables us to regain control of our minds.

Thought is part of the phenomenon, which is what the mind produces as the result of various factors. Thoughts appear and dissolve simultaneously, and the instant a thought arises it vanishes. Therefore, it is unnecessary to worry about how to eliminate thoughts. The essence of the Mind is emptiness, where nothing can be sustained. Thoughts come and go, never for a moment remaining in the Mind. But human beings tend to perceive a phenomenon and respond to it with our definitions and deluded thoughts. To chase phenomena with delusions only perpetuates the emergence of wandering thoughts. The mind perceives that wandering thoughts persist because it continually gives rise to thoughts. To halt this cycle of continuous thought generation, we must learn to stop the emergence of habitual thoughts and become the master of our own mind. As the master, we can consciously open new doors in life, ushering in fresh connections and opportunities.

The common challenge shared by beginning students is their attempt to avoid wandering thoughts. Purposely rejecting or suppressing thoughts only triggers more wandering thoughts. The proper remedy to use to eradicate wandering thoughts is to allow them to come and go on their own. Simply cease to pay attention to (or dance with) them. Instead, focus exclusively on practicing and maintaining the meditation method. Remain calm, tranquil and clear in your mind, and eventually the wandering thoughts will fade away by themselves. This will allow the Mind's innate clarity to become manifest.

Because it is critical to become the master of the mind, we should engage in meditation practice and cultivate the ability to consciously direct our thoughts. To transform thoughts is to focus on the method while remaining undisturbed by wandering thoughts. The energy that is normally given to unconscious thinking is redirected toward the conscious application of the method. The foundation of any spiritual practice is the application of a method in order to transform the scattered, wandering thoughts into a focused effort on the method, which is called the "single-pointed placement of the mind."

Following the cessation of wandering thoughts, we can bring forth mindful awareness and clarity. Through the absence of delusion due to the concentrated and inwardly directed awareness that shatters attachment, the mind will penetrate layer after layer of mental conditioning and reverse the flow of birth and death, thereby illuminating the Source of thought.

The Source of thought is our Original Nature, the Buddha Nature and the Original Face of the Mind. Given the right timing and supporting conditions, with one push the final layer of self-attachment can be broken. In that instance the subject and object reunite, and the individual directly experiences his essential, indivisible oneness with the universe, being born from the same essence. The Buddha and beings are of the same essence, and the unconditional loving kindness and compassion are manifested. But alas, by realizing the Way—with the Original Mind illuminated, the Original Nature seen—only half the journey has been completed. The practitioner must then continue to nurture and mature his realization until the precious Light grows and illuminates the entire universe, whereupon he can be the Teacher of Heaven and Men, re-entering the world on the Sail of Compassion in order to deliver all beings from suffering. No method that can support the attainment of enlightenment can transcend this path.

Regardless of the level of consciousness from which thoughts arise—whether it is deep or merely on the surface—it is an indisputable fact that no one but the thinker can create these thoughts. We are the sole creator and owner of our thoughts. If this fact is not acknowledged, we allow ourselves to become enslaved by our habits. This is why the practice of meditation is of the utmost importance. It helps us recognize wandering, scattered thoughts so they can be dissolved. Furthermore, once the light of awareness is able to penetrate the depth of subconscious activity, we can consciously give rise to beneficial thoughts that transform the mind and increase our awareness of the content of his consciousness, eventually leading to the destruction of I-consciousness and self-mastery. Then, we are finally the true owner of our life.

## Spiritual Suffering Is a Temporary Phenomenon

Change is not easy. Before we can meet our true self—the Pure Mind—self-attachment will remain the greatest enemy. Man always goes along with his habits, opening doors to significant harm. When challenging the habitual functioning pattern of the false self, we will experience mental and physical awkwardness and discomfort. Additionally, we can experience other vexations due to eagerness and the over-exertion of effort in his attempt to challenge and dissolve our own attachments. These are common reactions that arise from meditation, because the habitual path of self-attachment's functioning has been severed.

The claim that meditation can bring immediate pleasure and comfort—even going so far as to advocate practicing while lying down, leaning back in a seat or listening to music—misses the essence. It would be unusual for beginning students to experience physical relaxation or mental calm right away. It is a fact that when a practitioner confronts his self-attachment, a noticeable increase in mental and physical discomfort may occur. This is part of the process of meditation.

Initially, for a meditation session as short as five minutes you should not necessarily experience mental calm. On the contrary, some physical discomfort may occur. The most frequently experienced physical sensations are soreness, numbness or pain in the knees, legs and ankles, because in that moment your attachment to the physical body is being challenged. Practice bearing the discomfort and remain undisturbed by pain. As you become accustomed to this, you can gradually increase the length of the meditation sessions.

If the mind can focus on the method, it will gradually let go of its attachment to the physical body, whereupon the painful sensations will vanish. However, if you stop practicing due to the fear of pain, your mental attachment to the physical body will persist. Therefore, when practicing meditation, try to be at ease while maintaining a firm determination to successfully endure the period of discomfort.

The obstacles triggered through such effort are actually beneficial to the growth and maturation of the spirit. It is said that "crisis is the opportunity for change," but we must seize the opportunity. When practicing meditation, do not fear pain, because by going through it the obstacle can be overcome and changed. Growth is always accompanied by at least a little pain.

The initial goal of meditation is the clearing of mental afflictions in order to live a better life. But if you maintain the status quo, using your habitual pattern of belief and thinking in daily life, change cannot take place. Most people seek a life of leisure and joy, a life without stress and struggle. However, most of the time they tolerate suffering and lack the ability to choose otherwise.

Whether you are spiritual or not, whether or not you are wealthy or of respectable status, suffering and dissatisfaction are the unavoidable experience of all human beings. Suffering is caused by attachments and habitual tendencies that manifest as obstacles in your physical body and environment. Living necessarily comes with suffering, since man is surrounded by and constantly under the oppression of his scattered, wandering thoughts, which prevent him from reconnecting with the peace and harmony that is innately his to enjoy.

Most people believe they are able to manage their lives. If that is so, they ought to be able to have the thoughts they want and release the thoughts they do not want. Otherwise, there is really no control over the direction in which their lives are headed. Thoughts do not originate from outside the individual, nor can another person's thoughts become our own. To create the desired life, we must be able to give rise to the right thoughts. The idea is clear enough but not easy to accomplish, so it takes a great deal of effort. However, you must commit yourself to achieving it because otherwise more suffering will follow. Meditation is an effective method for calming your mind so you can consciously generate the right thoughts.

It is said that "you reap what you sow." If you succeed in deconstructing your unconscious mode of functioning, you will one day harvest and enjoy wonderful results. The time it takes for the results to manifest varies with the individual and the degree of effort. For some of you, a single word of wisdom can effect great change, while others may take an hour of practice to experience a positive shift. Some may require months or years of practice, or even longer, before substantial progress is made. In the spiritual journey, temporary encounters with discomfort and challenges are inevitable. In these moments of struggle, keep in mind that the suffering in spiritual practice is only temporary and will ultimately lead to the permanent eradication of the roots of suffering. While going through a life of the mundane, you experience an endless cycle of suffering.

In order to cut off the incessant flow of birth and death, it is necessary to start practicing with the right views and the right method, earnestly applying the principle of Zen in daily life. When you feel apprehensive about making changes and the difficulty of challenges, practice forbearance by looking forward to a bright future. After all, it is within your power to create that future.

Through unyielding determination to see the end of suffering, you will be liberated from the cycle of reincarnation. Through continual effort and practice, all problems can be resolved in this lifetime.

## The Present Moment Is the Only Truth

The techniques prescribed by various meditation practices may be different, but the important thing is whether they are able to clear away wandering thoughts and reveal the innate purity of the Mind. Through the diligent and correct application of such a method, you can deconstruct your unconscious mind functioning and experience the Pure Mind. Then you will see the reality and actualize the universal principle in your life. This is the third phase of Zen training, where the practitioner truly "sees the mountain again as mountain, sees the water again as water." At this stage, the practitioner's experiential understanding of the truth differs from that of the previous two stages.

In the initial stage, the definition created by the mind is applied to the mountain and water. But, at that point, the practitioner does not truly, purely perceive the real mountain and water. Then, in the second stage, having recognized the need to relinquish his definitions in order to perceive the absolute truth, he begins to doubt and inquire into the validity of his own definitions of reality. Without these definitions, his perception of reality will not be distorted, so he can challenge his own view of reality.

Finally, in the third stage, the practitioner no longer doubts himself. He has already cleared away the old, useless definitions of reality. As a result, the Mind's innate essence and functions are clearly manifested in his perception of reality. At this stage, the Mind is a clear, unclouded mirror that is able to present the truth without fault, being free of the defilement of distinctions and the grasping of phenomena. This is the stage at which the original nature of the Mind becomes manifest: *Beyond the shaded willow and bright flowers is yet another village*. This is what the Zen practitioners refer to as enlightenment.

I was once asked the question, "According to Zen, we should put away our attachments and definitions, but then what else is left?" If reality is presented without definitions, it is the truth. When we set aside all understanding of reality based on our old ways of reasoning and our deluded distinctions, the truth will become manifest. The truth will not disappear due to the absence of wandering thoughts and distinctions. It is the Mind's most authentic function.

As you read this book, if you can refrain from applying any definition or judgment regarding what has been written and not give rise to any wandering thoughts, then you are alive in this very moment. Thus you are directly interacting with reality, which is the present moment. You do not need to define your experience in this present moment, because reality does not require your judgment or definition in order to be so. It is already as manifested. To see the truth while maintaining a clear, peaceful mind—so that from emptiness awareness will emerge, whereupon awareness will illuminate the emptiness—is the training of the third stage: *seeing the mountain as mountain, seeing the water as water.*

Sitting with broken legs, mind scattered like swirling rain,

Sore, numb, bloated and aching, hammering

through barrier after barrier,

Why can he but I cannot? That is nonsense, illogical!

Determined shall I continue to sit, another round of

struggle goes on.

Gradually the mind and body cool, the ox's head

seems vaguely perceptible,

Two minds arising from phenomena, trembling is the

joyous thought,

Toss aside family and life, ignore the green wild flowers,

Strive to the gate at the end, from great dream one

shall awaken.

# 8 THE TRUTH IS WHERE IT STANDS

In front of the mountain, the ocean of yellow flowers is colorful,

Behind the hills, the white silver grass field spans the sky;

Splashing against the rock's crevices,

a place of refuge and rest,

Summoning the wind and rain, pearly smoke descended.

Approximately thirteen hundred years ago, in the Tang Dynasty, a practitioner called Mazu Daoyi meditated each day, trying to attain enlightenment. His teacher, the enlightened Master Nan-Yue Hui-Rang, recognized Mazu's capacity as a dharma vessel and therefore wanted to help him achieve a breakthrough by pointing out instructions. One day, he went to the place where Mazu meditated and asked him, "Practitioner, what do you seek by meditating?" Mazu replied, "To become the Buddha." Nan-Yue then found a piece of brick outside Mazu's hut and started grinding it against a rock.

Puzzled, Mazu asked, "Why are you grinding?" Nan-Yue said, "To make a mirror." Mazu questioned him, "How can grinding a brick make a mirror?!" Nan-Yue then said, "Since grinding a brick cannot make a mirror, how could sitting all day make a Buddha?"

Nan-Yue then went on to instruct him: *"Are you practicing seated Zen or seated Buddha? If practicing seated Zen, Zen is neither sitting nor lying down; if practicing seated Buddha, Buddha is without fixed form.*

For the dharma is without abiding, there shall be neither accepting nor rejecting. If you try to be seated Buddha, you are killing the Buddha; if you are obsessed with the form of sitting, you have not attained the understanding." For Mazu, having heard Nan-Yue's teaching, it was as if the heavenly elixir had filled his body through the top of his head.

The Zen approach to teaching seizes the magic of the moment to directly point out the nature of the Mind in order to help a practitioner cast off his attachments and sweep aside the cloud to reveal the Light. Zen directly points out the attachment as it operates in the moment, for the Buddha has no fixed form and the illness of the mind is attachment. It directly points out the Mind's function, for the present moment is as it is; it directly points out the essence of the Mind, for the reunification with the primordial truth. As master Yongjia said, "*Cutting straight to the Source as affirmed by the Buddhas, picking the leaves and branches however I cannot.*"

## Cultivation in the Movement of Daily Life

The term "Mind" in Zen teaching refers to the Buddha Nature, Bodhicitta, the Source of all existence, or the First Cause of life. The innate essence and capacity of the Mind are all-pervasive and unaffected by any attachment or mental defilement. Defilement and attachment can obscure the primordial wisdom and Light of the Mind but cannot annihilate its essential nature. Because the Mind is primordial, it transcends the limitation of conditional arising and exists without other factors. When the Mind is obscured by self-attachment, it is impure. The Pure Mind is one that is free from the contamination of self-attachment and delusion.

A mind that is free of attachment and delusion is the Buddha; it can manifest the authentic functioning of the Mind, which is the Way, the Right Way or the Buddha Way. The Pure Mind is the Buddha, and the Buddha is the Pure Mind. Those who attain the Way realize the true essence of the Mind and are therefore able to function from this Pure Mind in daily life.

The Pure Mind's functioning is authentic functioning. It is beyond right and wrong, beyond coming and going, beyond past and present, beyond faces and eyes, beyond the holy and the mundane, beyond male or female, and beyond defilement or purity. It is everlasting and luminous just as it is, with nothing extra. For those who know, it is the wondrous creation of the Mind; the ignorant have called it "ghost" or "spirit." The poet Li Bai wrote: "*Today's men do not see the ancient moon, yet today's moon has shone on ancient men; ancient men and today's men are like flowing water, yet the bright moon they saw has stayed the same.*" The bright moon is empty of intent, so it can illuminate both the past and present; when the bright moon is present, the blue is blue, yellow is yellow and white is white. However, the moon is not blue, yellow or white.

Authentic practice is not confined to meditation, Zen inquiry, contemplation of Buddha, recitation of scripture, mantra practice with visualization and mudra, or prostration and repentance. It encompasses every instance of mind functioning that arises in daily life. We walk the spiritual path continually in our lives, cultivating it in our daily encounters, in every aspect of life, in each moment of thought arising that presents us with the opportunity to train the mind.

Zen Master Shi-Tou Xi-Qian asked the layman Pang, "Since the day you came to see me, how have you handled daily matters?" Layman Pang presented the following verse:

> *In daily life, there is no particular chore,*
> *Just whatever naturally comes to me.*
> *No grasping, no rejecting;*
> *No commotion, no blundering.*
> *Red and purple, none the better,*
> *Mountains and hills, not a speckle of dust.*
> *Supernatural magic and marvelous activities—*
> *Carrying water and gathering wood.*

This koan presents the Zen concept of "minding the foot-steps:" being mindful of every instance of mind functioning, because each instance is the point at which life takes a step.

The effort made in Buddhist practices is a minor effort, but the real effort is to give rise to mindful awareness in daily life and dispel attachments through wakefulness. We must fully employ the foundation established in our minor effort by bringing it into the major effort of our life so that it can make a real difference. Master Lin-Ji said:

> *There is no particular place for making efforts in Buddha dharma*
> *other than the ordinary: passing dung, spewing urine, putting on*
> *clothes, eating meals and lying down when tired. The fools laughed*

*at me, but the wise knew. The ancients said, 'To work on the outside is always the stubborn fool.' Just be your own master wherever you are, then the truth is already where it stands; phenomenon is not to be exchanged. Even within the habitual tendencies, the five non-ceasing karmas, therein lies the oceanic liberation.*

The ultimate goal of Buddha dharma is to expound and reveal the universal truth: the principle realized by the Buddha, the Awakened One. The principle realized by the Buddha is not the understanding of an ordinary being. Familiarizing himself with the right view, the ordinary being begins to substitute the Buddha's view for his own. As he familiarizes himself with this new way of seeing, he will effect subtle transformation. Given the inertia of countless eons of habitual accumulation, change cannot occur instantly. It is necessary to break down the habitual tendencies with various methods, which have been developed through many teachings and countless hours of practice.

Worldly understanding is not the ultimate truth, and trying to understand the ultimate truth through the ordinary being's conceptualization completely misses the point. The ordinary being's understanding is based on attachment, but the ultimate truth is emptiness; the ordinary being's understanding is relative and dualistic, but the ultimate truth is absolute and non-dualistic; the ordinary being's understanding is based on discriminating consciousness, but the ultimate truth is the wisdom of the whole; the ordinary being's understanding is the cause of suffering, but the ultimate truth is the cause of liberation.

If we cannot skillfully utilize the Buddha dharma as the remedy for our problems, then we may find ourselves in danger of developing attachment to the teachings and becoming trapped in the vast ocean of philosophical knowledge, unable to benefit from the teachings because we are lost in the tides of philosophical debate and argument. This is not the fault of the Buddha; it is the result of the attachments developed within the student. We must recognize this pitfall, for if we practice Buddha's teaching this way, even if a thousand Buddhas were to appear it would not be helpful.

## Buddhism Teaches Self-Help

Truth, being the universal principle or the way of the Pure Mind, is always present in daily life. The truth is indestructible and unavoidable, because it governs the operation of every form of existence in the universe. However, the realization of the universal principle is only possible through the experience of enlightenment: the realization of the essence of the Mind. Otherwise, one cannot understand how the universal principle actually affects each aspect of one's life. Thoughts and behaviors arising from a defiled mind cannot conform to the universal principle, so unconsciously they create problems for the individual.

Ordinary beings are ignorant of the universal principle, but the enlightened saints have been able to live life according to these principles. The following story illustrates the difference between ordinary beings and enlightened beings:

One of Master Huihai's disciples once asked him, "Master, in cultivating the Way, do you still practice?"

Master replied, "I practice." Then the disciple asked, "How do you practice?"

Master said, "Eat when hungry, rest when sleepy."

The disciple was puzzled. Everyone does that, so how can it be considered practice? He pursued the question: "Since most people do the same thing, is the master's practice any different?"

Huihai replied, "It is different."

"How is it different?" the disciple asked

*"Others don't eat when it is time to eat. Instead, they have hundreds of desires and needs. They don't sleep when it is time, but instead they have thousands of complaints and demands. Such is the difference."*

Enlightened beings do not entertain deluded thoughts while eating, but ordinary beings experience a barrage of wandering thoughts, from which they discriminate according to their tastes. Ordinary beings get caught up with these distinctions. When sleeping, the enlightened being's awareness is still present, but most ordinary beings continue with wandering thoughts in their sleep, often experiencing nightmares and the inability to rest. The mind of the ordinary being is constantly grasping phenomenon without a moment of rest. This is the main difference.

The Four Great Aspirations of a bodhisattva are:

*Sentient Beings boundless, I vow to save,*

*Vexations inexhaustible, I vow to sever,*

*Dharma immeasurable, I vow to learn,*

*Buddhahood unsurpassable, I vow to attain.*

White Cloud Zen Master also had four aspirations:

*When hungry I shall eat,*
*When cold I wear more clothes,*
*When tired I stretch out and sleep,*
*When hot I enjoy the blowing breeze.*

The mind has the same potential, whether or not it is enlightened. Due to the different ways in which the individual makes use of his mind, different results will be manifested.

Sakyamuni Buddha was not the creator of the universal truth. He merely taught his students how to realize the truth and liberate themselves from the deluded life of ignorance in order to become their own Buddha. Sakyamuni Buddha recognized the contradiction between people's desire to attain liberation through the traditional Brahman religion and the suffering inherent in the caste system that was part of the tradition. For many of today's religions, having strayed from the essential message of compassion and wisdom, their methods of practice and essential goal of dissolving attachments become diluted and nebulous, creating arguments and contradictions among individuals and religious or ethnic groups.

The historic Buddha, having realized the flaws in many religions and methods of practice in his time, and intending to seek understanding and solutions for the cause of suffering in birth, aging, illness and death, took leave of family in order to commit himself to a spiritual journey. Through his diligent effort he attained the complete, perfect enlightenment of the truth, and his life became a perfect expression of the truth. The Buddha's teaching is handed from one generation to the next in order to resolve the practical issues that humanity faces in life, not to be enshrined as some impractical, highbrow philosophy. The original intent of Sakyamuni Buddha was not to create an organized religion. He taught only for the sake of showing sentient beings how to liberate themselves from suffering. The formation of organized practice and teaching came later, in order to meet the need to sustain the teaching through the changes that occurred with respect to time, place and social circumstance.

As the Buddha realized, the truth was able to dissolve vexations and lead sentient beings away from suffering toward happiness. Because all problems result from the unskillful use of the mind, the direct spiritual path is to dissolve the faulty mental habits in order to reveal the true nature of the Mind. To seek an alternate path of liberation while ignoring the consequences of self-attachment is a common error among today's spiritual seekers. Beliefs, personality and physical body are the concrete presentations of an individual's self-attachment. Together, they are the foundation for the attainment of enlightenment, but they are also the biggest obstacle, the source of all suffering. Ignoring this reality, no one can effectively resolve life's many practical problems, much less attain enlightenment.

It was not the Buddha's intention that sentient beings should ignore their lives. In fact, his pursuit and attainment of truth was motivated by the aspiration to solve the most practical and real problems of birth, aging, illness and death. Therefore, to discuss Buddha's teaching separately from those problems is to completely miss the point and deviate from the essential principle of existence. By overlooking the true intent of the Buddha's teaching, the practitioner will remain trapped in the suffering of samsara, which is the greatest obstacle to spiritual progress for today's practitioner. Without a genuine motivation to solve the problems of birth, aging, illness and death, man will be caught in suffering. Without a sincere motivation in regard to the truth, man will remain in ignorance.

Buddha Sakyamuni was the founder of Buddhism, but he did not come as a rescuer of sentient beings. Instead, he came as a teacher who showed us all how to save ourselves. Seated meditation is a tool for eliminating delusion; but, as illustrated by the case of Nan-Yue and Mazu, without the right view meditation cannot restore the mind to its mirror-like clarity. The phenomena we experience are influenced by our view. To benefit from practice, you must first establish yourself in the right view, instead of mistaking the result for the cause.

Let us consider this example: When a person goes out on the street, the path he takes and the scenery he experiences are mostly determined by his own inclinations and desires. Similarly, when a person meditates, the phenomena and physical or mental experiences in terms of feelings and sensations are also largely determined by his spiritual view, or his idea of what reality is. Wherever the Mind is, the phenomenon is; the observer's position already determines what will be observed. We should not try to pursue and grasp phenomena, but should instead inquire within ourselves as to whether we possess the ability to manifest, from our mind, the desired phenomena for our life.

It is said in Zen, "*The wise discipline the mind, the fools pursue phenomena.*" It is also said, "*The giant is ignorant of the jewel on his forehead, therefore he seeks outside himself.*" Our thought is the observer, and the phenomenon corresponding to that thought is the observed object. To make a change, we cannot mistake the result for the cause, or our effort will be fruitless. When the view of the Pure Mind cannot be manifested, it is because of delusional tendencies. In the vast ocean of thoughts, we need a guiding compass in order to reach the other shore. This guiding compass is the right view that points inwardly toward the mind and serves as an antidote to the attachment.

## Life as Image in the Mirror

The Pure Mind has two chief characteristics, namely emptiness and awareness. The Mind can function and encompass all existence, but nothing exists outside the Mind. To see and be seen, to hear and be heard, to feel and be felt, to think and be thought of are all results of the Mind's functioning, and all existences are created by and contained in the Mind. When we are able to abide in the Mind's emptiness and awareness, we can then attain a complete understanding of this concept. When we find and rest at ease in the Pure Mind, the eternity of Life will become manifest and the innate wisdom of the Mind will naturally emerge.

The formless Pure Mind is the source of Life. It is the "*sign of imperceptible summit:*" one of the thirty-two marks of perfect awakening of the Buddha's physical body manifestations. The Pure Mind can manifest all phenomena and all functions, so it is the *"power of Samantabhadra engaging in the activities of the Tathagata."* The Pure Mind can enter all phenomena and function without confusion, so it is the *"wisdom of Manjushri that destroys all attachments."* The Pure Mind is all-knowing and all-perceiving in regard to every phenomenon and function, so it is the *"compassion of Avalokiteshvara, hearing and rescuing all beings from suffering."* The Pure Mind gives rise to all functions, manifesting all forms in the present moment, so it is the *"coming of the Venerated Maitreya Buddha."* The Pure Mind's ability to encompass all functions and forms is boundless, so it is the *"Bodhisattva of Boundless Body."*

A common misperception of *emptiness* equates it to nothingness, or the absence of phenomena and thoughts and the opposite of existence. This understanding of what emptiness really means is incorrect. When people misinterpret an unconscious state of mind—one in which the individual is unaware of wandering thoughts—as a state of emptiness, they fail to recognize that this experience of emptiness is a manufactured one created by their own thoughts. It is not the true emptiness of the Mind.

We must remember that feeling is just a thought, so without the presence of a thought to correspond to the feeling, we will not experience anything. The so-called *emptiness* created by an individual thought is relative and belongs to the realm of the birth-and-death dichotomy. It is not the essential emptiness that transcends the duality of phenomenon's birth-death. The Mind is formless, tranquil and motionless, neither created nor destroyed, neither coming nor going. Moreover, its innate awareness is always present and encompasses all phenomena corresponding to each instance of mind functioning.

Various forms are created within this emptiness-awareness, so emptiness is not different from other forms. The forms that are manifested, which correspond to each instance of mind functioning, are inseparable from the emptiness-awareness nature of the Mind, so form is not different from emptiness. Through the essence of emptiness, the mind manifests forms, becoming aware of forms through innate awareness and illuminating forms through innate luminosity. Emptiness is formless, awareness is formless, and luminosity is also formless. All forms are self-liberated, manifesting form while being essentially formless. Form is selfless, so in essence it is not form. The empty mind is capable of functioning and is therefore formless while manifesting form. Because it does not belong to subject-object duality but is capable of functioning through non-dualistic subject-object relationships, the Mind is inconceivably, unimaginably subtle and profound.

The Pure Mind possesses the nature of emptiness, but it is also the luminous awareness, the omniscient and the complete clarity. While the Mind is emptiness, it is also aware, and it is able to give birth to all forms and manifestations. With regard to the Pure Mind, emptiness and awareness are simply two aspects of a single essence.

The nature of emptiness is similar to the selfless clarity of a mirror: There is no fixed image in the mirror; the clarity is awareness, and selflessness is the emptiness. The function of the mirror is to present the truth without grasping the images. It does not have the capacity to grasp them. The Mind's emptiness-clarity is like the mirror: It can give rise to any function without holding onto it. Essentially, the Mind always has emptiness-clarity, awareness and luminosity, and it is always in the present moment, functioning and manifesting dependently arising phenomena. But, when the phenomenon is gone, no trace is left behind. The arising exists simultaneously with the disappearance of causal and supportive factors.

The instant of the Mind's functioning, the perception, presentation and formation of phenomena arise from its emptiness. This emptiness has no fixed form and is beyond grasping; it only responds to factors and conditions. The essence of the Mind is awareness and emptiness; therefore, when the Mind functions according to a certain pattern, it is aware of that functioning, just as whenever a person enters or exits the front door of a house the resident owner of the house will inevitably become aware of that person. The absence of such awareness is ignorance, which results from one's attachment to unconscious mind functioning. If, in the instance of functioning, we give rise to phenomena with innate awareness, we are in the state of liberation, a state of awakening and self-ease.

The process of the Mind's functioning is similar to the creation of a virtual reality: To achieve this virtual reality, software must be developed and entered into the computer, which then constructs a simulated reality according to the program so that the individual—the user of this virtual reality—can interact with it and derive various experiences.

A sentient being is like the computer programmer who has developed the original software, the pattern of thought creation. The computer can then manifest the interactive phenomena and the simulated reality, the Mind manifesting the result of an instance of mind functioning as the reality. The user of the program will then experience this illusory reality, the situation and phenomena encountered by sentient beings on a daily basis. The Mind gives rise to thoughts and reflects the results of the thoughts in the individual's reality. The pattern of thought creation determines the reality experienced by the individual and his modality of functioning. Not simply a belief or theory, it is, without exception, a universal truth.

Awareness is the other essential characteristic of the Mind. Awareness and emptiness are inseparable: In the presence of true emptiness there is innate awareness, so the presence of innate awareness is accompanied by true emptiness. Awareness means the Mind is aware of all phenomenal realms and functions that arise from and are encompassed by the nature of the Mind as emptiness. This primordial awareness is boundless, and nothing can transcend it. All phenomena—this world and the entire universe, and the different levels of phenomenal realms—are within the bounds of this innate awareness, because the Mind is omniscient. Outside the Mind, there are no phenomena, while outside the phenomena there is no Mind.

The Mind functions in different directions according to various patterns of functioning. Similar thoughts resonate with similar energy aggregates. The structural density of such aggregates is dependent on the strength of attachment, and it forms the myriad multiple-layered phenomenal realms that are mutually dependent and support each other as causes and results. Thought arises from the emptiness of the Mind; its source is the root of Life. If thoughts can be likened to seeds or primitive computer programs, we must say that every aspect and facet of existence is an extension of thought. Existence includes our thought, the physical body, the environment and all of life's situations. Existence is entirely a composition of energy and a presentation of the Mind's functioning.

The Mind is formless. Similarly, a person's "ability to do something" is formless because it cannot be recognized until a tangible result of that action takes form. For example, to see whether someone is indeed a good artist, one must examine his artistic creation instead of merely considering the person's appearance. The Mind, formless and imperceptible, can manifest all phenomena and forms.

The Mind's experience of phenomenan is like an image in the mirror, neither going nor coming, neither increasing nor decreasing. It is lucid and forever tranquil. Emptiness, awareness and the phenomenon are actually one indivisible whole called existence. Existence is demonstrated through emptiness, but emptiness becomes evident only through existence. The form of phenomenon depends upon the formless essence in order to manifest its own existence. Moreover, the formless essence can only demonstrate its nature and functioning through the manifestation of form. This is the meaning behind a well-known statement in *Heart Sutra*: "*Form is emptiness, emptiness is form.*" Emptiness and existence are non-dualistic, as are emptiness and awareness.

Awareness exists when thought arises. Emptiness is also there, arising and dissolving simultaneously. The Mind is lucid, but in its emptiness it is tranquil. When the reality of daily life becomes manifest from the nature of the Mind as emptiness, the Mind's innate awareness is clear and sharp in its knowing, completely and clearly aware of the entire process, being the appearance and disappearance of thought and the appearance and disappearance of connected phenomena. This subtle but very important truth can only be realized and affirmed through direct experience.

"*Lying the body across the universe*": This means the enlightened masters realize that awareness is all-pervasive throughout the Great Void, and that nothing exists outside this emptiness-awareness. A poem describing the experience of enlightenment said, "*With one punch the Great Void is broken through, billions of Mt. Merus vanish without a trace. Tell me in all this who is the master? A sphere of red light has sprung up from the East.*" This is a statement of the most authentic truth, not poetic analogy.

In the enlightenment experience, we directly experience the innate clarity and emptiness of the Mind as truly pervading all space and all phenomenal realms. The question of how long a practitioner can remain in this perception of his original nature will depend on the depth to which his attachments have been eradicated. The deeper he can go to clear away the attachments, the longer he can abide in this innate emptiness-awareness. If the accumulation of attachment is still quite strong, the experience of enlightenment cannot be sustained for longer than a minute. This is why, after the enlightenment experience, we must continue to nurture this singular purity. No matter the depth of an individual's realization, the task of sustained nurturing and maturation must continue. Otherwise, there is the danger that the force of past conditioning and defilements will cause him to regress back to his initial state of ignorance.

An enlightened individual is able to function through the emptiness and awareness of the Pure Mind. It is as if a blind person has recovered his sight and is again able to see the world clearly, setting his own direction toward the desired goal. Unfortunately, many people still do not know the right direction and destination in life because they have not made contact with their true self-nature. Instead, they stumble along a path filled with obstacles.

The ancients said, "*Clear in the essence, eating and drinking are all for the benefit and health of one's being; ignorant in the mind, even Zen discourses and utterances are nothing than just meaningless manipulations of consciousness.*" Unless one becomes enlightened to the nature of the Mind, he will be unable to function from the purity of emptiness and awareness. Consequently, he will live like the blind and deaf, knowing neither where he came from nor where he is going. Life is the creation of the Mind, but thoughts are the tools of the Mind. Whenever we experience vexations and worries, it is an indication that we have not given rise to the right thoughts, but have instead focused our energy in the wrong place. As long as our thoughts remain in the wrong place, our encounters will also remain in the wrong place.

## Toil for Whom? Busy for Whom?

The understanding and acceptance of reality marks the true beginning of change. If the individual has not yet recognized that he cultivates each moment of life through his thoughts, and if he fails to understand the principle of cause and effect, then he will be constantly surprised by the outcome of his efforts. To truly engage in spiritual practice, we must be mindful of how we use our mind at every level and in each aspect of life. Whether awake or not, we must have the ability to consciously notice and transform the emergence of thoughts.

A human being gives rise to countless thoughts in his sleep, but how many thoughts can he actually remember after waking up in the morning? Most remember only the bare minimum or sometimes nothing at all. In the lethargic state of sleep, man completely surrenders his will to involuntary, unconscious thinking habits. Master Xuefeng said, *"A lone lamp illuminating the night stand, taking off shoes and socks one climbed in bed, three spirits and seven souls gone in the dreams, return or not in the morning remain untold."* When we are unable to master the mind's functioning, we have no leverage to effect change and must drift along with the flow of karma.

According to the sutra, *"Reality manifests according to karma, the individual experiences results through his karma."* We must cultivate the habit of observing our own mental pattern of functioning and inwardly shine the light of awareness upon the Mind. The moment-to-moment illumination of the mind renders the unconscious functioning powerless to operate, so we must elevate the relative control we possesses over the process of thought creation. Illumination of the Mind should be practiced to the point where there is neither the illuminator nor the illuminated, at which point the practitioner will be able to penetrate to the True Illumination of the Middle Way. All practices must follow this process of Mind Illumination in order to be established as cultivatable, verifiable and practical.

The basis of life's instability is delusion. This is the extension of an individual's I-consciousness, which is inherently ignorant. Due to attachment, an individual constructs a false I-consciousness and plans how to live out his life through this false "I"-dentity, so that his family, career, spirituality and other aspects are contained within the deluded confines of the I-consciousness.

The footprint of life's unfolding is simply the course of the Mind's manifestations. From early childhood to adulthood, human beings plan every moment of life, but what else is there once these goals have been set? Whether the goals are attainable or not, the impermanence of life rolls on. The accomplishment of any goal is nothing but a temporary expansion of self-attachment, or at best a momentary satisfaction.

Life is in essence a series of continuous changes, and as such it is inherently unstable and restless. The poet Yuanming Tao wrote a poem somewhat appropriate to this point: "*Life is drifting and unstable, like the dust on the street; dispersed everywhere by the turning wind, this body is no longer the way it was.*" Life is an endlessly evolving process, so there is no end to be found in the past, the present or the future. Death is not the real conclusion of life, so it is only meaningful to talk about the refuge of life. The ultimate meaning—or the purpose—of life is to find its true refuge, and that singular point of refuge is the Mind. Having found the Mind, we can rest at ease and settle our life. We can manifest the unborn, undestroyed eternity of life.

Life, in the absence of this refuge, is fleeting and unstable. However, by functioning from the essence of the Mind an individual can be his own master wherever he is. Only a life that unfolds from the Pure Mind—which is the true refuge of the individual—will become the Way, thus leading to peace and returning the individual to his Source.

Life is a never-ending process, unlike the popular perception of life as a movie that always comes to an end. The innate Mind is eternal, unborn, undestroyed and always able to give rise to thoughts. Therefore, life will go on forever, whether in a cyclical existence driven by phenomena-grasping proliferation or in a life that is awakened, non-dualistic and eternal. By consciously giving rise to wholesome thoughts, one will gradually become able to take control of life. Life is holistic, and wealth and reputation do have important roles, but ultimately it is beyond fame and profit.

Some have believed that the happiness and fulfillment experienced by the wealthy are due only to the abundance of money, and they set for themselves the goal of acquiring large sums of money as a way to secure happiness. Such a goal is a delusion. The truth is that, in the pursuit of money, we must recognize that we are also acquiring the same suffering of the wealthy. It is not news that wealth and social power often lead to harmful karma that more than negate any benefits money could bring to our family, prosperity, reputation and health.

The ancients warned against the pursuit of profit by saying, *"Having collected nectars of hundreds of flowers to make the honey, toil for whom? Busy for whom?"* and *"Flying goose left just a trace of sand, man gone to the underworld only his name is left behind."* Fame and profit do not guarantee happiness. The only means to attain everlasting happiness is to cultivate the ability to generate thoughts of happiness and contentment. It means having the ability to manifest happiness and contentment as reality in our life. This kind of happiness and contentment is not delusory.

If an individual does not have self-awareness, he may ultimately carve a path of vexation and suffering in the pursuit of happiness. Therefore, in setting goals for life, be certain that such goals are real and beneficial. They should not be based on deluded perceptions, or you will unconsciously create more suffering.

Many people have said to me, "I am really diligent in my practice, so why are my relationships still so stressed?" In the result one can see the cause: Without the planting of certain seeds, there is no reason to expect the corresponding outcome. It is not useful to lament how things turn out in life; the reality is already here and should be recognized as such. We must remember that every situation we encounter is already the outcome, fruition and evidence of all our previous efforts. These situations are the end product we have created, the fruits of our habitual, unconscious thoughts.

The reality we face each day is of our own conscious or

unconscious making, because we are the sole creator of our fate. Zen Master Chang-Sha said, *"Most profound! Most profound! The phenomenal realm and body are the Mind. The ignorant confuses the Mind as form; in the instance of realization all becomes the True Mind."* In spiritual practice, the realization of the essence of the Mind is foremost. Having realized the Way, knowing that outside the Mind there is no phenomenon, the practitioner can abide in calmness, giving life a refuge of withdrawal; a real and peaceful dwelling in which to settle. To cultivate the Way is to abide and maintain the Way after enlightenment. Whether we are in motion, at rest, at leisure or in activity, we should never separate ourselves from the innate awareness of the Mind. Once all the supporting conditions have matured, then we can achieve the complete eradication of all delusion and truly actualize the Way.

The ancients said, *"Establishing the mind upon the Great Way, vexation naturally goes away."* For mankind today, it is sadly more appropriate to say, "Establishing the mind on vexations all day, the Great Way naturally goes away." The Way is the universal principle and the refuge of withdrawal for the individual; it is the manifestation of the Pure Mind and the non-dualistic union of man and his Creator. The Way is the actualization of unborn, undestroyed liberation. It is the law of life that applies equally to mundane life and spirituality.

To deviate from the Way, a person's actions must be contrary to the Way. Action that is contrary to the Way is the source of suffering. *"To seek a Way outside the Way, one will never meet the Way, hastily life shall pass, nothing but regret in the end."* To realize the Way, cultivate the Way and actualize the Way, never deviate from it. These are the practices of cultivation and fruition. Having the ability to realize the Way and practice the Way, we can stand in the truth wherever we are and become the master of our reality.

Han-Shan and Shi-De, two blissful saints,
Meeting each situation wherever they are
with playful songs;
Inseparably united in meaning just like Mung and Jiao,
The green mountain one may attain just where he stands.

# 9 RIDING THE OX HOME, HOME IS NOT

Under the Lin-Ji staff there are many dead,

The King of Hell decrees urgently their imprisonment;

Home-seeking spirits commanded by the Five Schools,

Summon the descendants to burn offerings at the tomb.


The individual who has the right views for life and the universe shall see suffering depart and will thus be free and at ease. It seems that most people think Buddhism places too much emphasis on suffering, as if to imply that life is nothing but suffering and Buddhism is only about getting rid of that suffering. Many people question Buddhism's, "What is the meaning of such a human life?" It is necessary to realize that suffering is an inevitable part of human experience. It is a fact that suffering exists in everyday life. It has been said that *"every family has a tough sutra to recite,"* meaning that each individual has his or her own suffering. Human history, whether ancient or recent, whether Chinese or not, tells us there have been and still are widespread diseases, natural disasters and many ongoing wars among social strata, countries and ethnic groups. On the personal level, there is the suffering of birth, aging, illness and the death of the physical body, as well as the suffering of vexation, attachment, arguments and judgments of right versus wrong, and the lack of control over our own thoughts. These, too, are part of suffering. These facts are present and occur continuously among the various nations and regions, as well as within each individual living today. The expression *"ten thousand household lamps, ten thousand vexations"* is true indeed.

Human beings have tried, through various means, to relieve all forms of suffering. This is true of the past, the present and in regard to what is anticipated for the future. The development of technology is intended to bring more convenience into our daily lives, and to relieve the suffering of mental and physical limitations in this physical world. The development of medicine is aimed at improving health so as to alleviate the pain and suffering of illness. The development of philosophy is for the purpose of guiding humanity through the suffering of cultural darkness, spiritual poverty and chaos. The development of education is intended to uplift humanity from the suffering of ignorance and the lack of skills for basic subsistence. The development of art is for the purpose of compensating the suffering in the perceived imperfection of Creation. The development of religion is for the release of humanity from the suffering of life's uncertainty in order to achieve liberation from birth, aging, illness and death, and to attain the ultimate goal of eternal life. It is clear that suffering is the motivating force behind all human endeavors, and suffering shall remain the significant focus of human existence.

The individual who lacks a long-term vision and consideration for the future has no choice but to be engrossed by immediate concerns and vexations. Externally, man's desire for physical sustenance includes food, heating oil and other economic resources; internally, he is oppressed by cravings for wealth, sensual pleasure, fame, taste and sleep. Given his preoccupation with these inner and outer desires, Man has no time left in which to reflect on the real problem he must resolve.

The lack of the right perspective regarding life and the correct understanding of the universal truth inevitably lead to the creation of all kinds of suffering. Man then either lives in suffering without the conscious recognition of his plight or is unable to extricate himself from suffering, even when he is able to recognize the gravity of the situation. If he then adopts the view that suffering is the "essential" and "normal" condition of life, he will lose the motivation to seek freedom. Consequently, suffering shall stay with him from one life to the next, as he resigns himself to pleasure-seeking activities, always oblivious to the underlying reality of suffering.

Sakyamuni Buddha, in his profound wisdom, clarified the truth of suffering. Through his unconditional compassion, he urged all beings to seek freedom from suffering. A happy and fulfilling life is the liberation from suffering in the conventional sense; complete freedom from a cyclical existence into the unborn, undestroyed essence is the liberation from suffering in the ultimate sense. Eternal life is the fruition of freedom from the vexation of life's uncertainty and instability. The impetus to seek this liberation is the basis of all human knowledge. It is the ultimate goal, not only of our spiritual pursuits but of our materialistic pursuits as well.

The eternity of life requires that we develop the deep recognition that a false sense of an independent "I" is the real cause of suffering. We must completely eradicate the unconscious mode of mind functioning built upon that false "I" in order to free ourselves from birth, aging, illness and death. In so doing we can realize the non-dualistic oneness of "I" and the world, the subject and the object, the individual and the Collective, man and his Creator, the agency of functioning and its recipient, and the state of cyclical existence and the unborn state of liberation. The actualization of the universal principle and truth in our life is the ultimate state of liberation from suffering. It is the completion of eternal life.

## Wisdom Leading to the Experiential Understanding of Life

A successful relationship requires common sense, the investigation of science requires knowledge, and the cultivation of a bright future requires the correct perspective on life. The experiential understanding of life requires wisdom, which is the right view based on the understanding of the universal principles. Our view is the navigator of our life, so without the right view we will not only fail to attain the freedom of an unborn, undestroyed state but will also come away from our worldly endeavors empty-handed. Regardless of whatever situation we face in life, it is nothing other than the concrete evidence of the karma created by our own view; the manifestation and extension of phenomena resonating with our own pattern of mind functioning.

The *Shurangama Sutra* states, *"In the Treasury of the Tathagata, the nature of form is true emptiness, and the nature of emptiness is true form; innately pure and pervading the Dharma Realms. Through sentient beings' minds, in response to their capacity to know, reality manifests according to beings' karma."* The mind of true emptiness is all-pervasive in the dharma realms, and sentient beings create their own karma through this mind functioning. Therefore, our reality and experience of life shall occur according to our karma. Each person's reality is exactly the karma that he has created and must therefore bear. It is neither more nor less. This is why each individual lives a completely unique life. In the moment of mind functioning, the individual's habitual tendency demonstrates its power, and the habit that is cultivated by the false "I" sets the direction in which his karma will mature.

Independence and the respect for life have become the trend in mainstream society as the means by which to emphasize and encourage individuality. For example, respect for human rights, gender equality and the protection of animals have been focal points of social attention. Led onward by the collective thinking of today, modern man has pursued the fantasy of complete, unrestrained freedom, seeking to break through the physical limitations of the human body and his intellectual capacity. Today's education is focused on the strengthening of the individual's I-consciousness as a means to protect the individual's right to the pursuit of happiness and the avoidance of suffering. Popular culture values eccentricity in fashions and behaviors, all being designed for the purpose of self-exhibition. Any unusual style or action that exaggerates an individual's persona and differentiates that individual from the rest is deemed to be "cool."

Such social phenomena are the creation and direction of the collective consciousness of our time; they are the results of shared karma. Politics, economics, education, technology and religion are also factors in that trend. Once a certain path has been anointed as the right one, whether or not the intention is clear, society at large tends to follow that path toward an unknown future, guided by beliefs conceived through the flawed I-consciousness. Humanity has become the lab rat for conducting experiments on various beliefs, philosophies and social systems. Thus the experimentation and failure of a flawed system place a burden on society, while the social trend drives the individual in the direction indicated by the collective thinking. But be cautious: This trend is a one-way street with no turning back.

Today's educational system molds the individual's sense of self; it emphasizes the sense of self. The over-emphasis of self and the neglect of the Collective is at the expense of an increased burden and conflict that perpetuate the dualistic perception of reality, further paralyzing the already rigid boundary that defines people as mutually incompatible.

On the other hand, if the emphasis is only on the Collective—on the need for withdrawing the individualistic proliferation in the wrong direction—this will hasten ignorance on the collective level. Many dictators in history have used religion as a means to solidify their political power, which is the improper guidance of spiritual withdrawal. The use of religion as a means to control the collective consciousness for selfish benefit not only violates the true spiritual message behind the religion, but it also incurs the ignorance of humanity.

The right refuge for spiritual withdrawal is respectful of the individual's uniqueness, while possessing a strong characteristic of restraint. The Mind is the Collective, and its nature is emptiness. Each thought, as it functions from the Mind, is different. This is the nature of uniqueness. While the Mind gives rise to all phenomena, all phenomena are different. This is also the nature of uniqueness. This nature of uniqueness actually makes evident the existence of the individual. For example, the saints of the Pure Land were liberated, selfless beings, but they possessed unique aspirations and merits. The enlightened beings realized that the nature of the Pure Mind is non-dualistic oneness, like water dissolving in water. The withdrawal of functioning is accomplished through the emptiness of the Mind, but each enlightened being can still manifest his or her individuality. The Pure Land is the Pure Mind, and the holy assembly of the Pure Land represents the vast diversity of functions of the Pure Mind. The enlightened individual withdraws into the essence of the non-dualistic Pure Land without losing the uniqueness of his individuality. Only the manifestations of individuality through the non-dualistic essence can be free of conflict: This is the only possible path by which to fulfill the future of humanity and life's eternity.

The recognition of suffering, which motivates the search for liberation and the understanding that the I-consciousness must be dissolved, is the only approach that should be encouraged as the right practice of spiritual withdrawal leading to eternal life and the dissolution of subject-object duality. To merge with the Collective without losing the individuality is genuine oneness. True freedom, or independence, is respectful of the individual. It does not interfere with the withdrawal of the individual into the Collective, nor does it create the side effects of over-emphasizing individualism. In this way, the blind spot of society can be lifted and its burden relieved, as humanity marches toward a new culture that completes its pursuits in order to fulfill life's eternity.

The emphasis on individualism creates more chaos in the world of duality. The method of scientific analysis presumes the individual to be the absolute observer, which further accentuates the sense of a separate "I." Even the smallest, subtlest form of I-consciousness cannot integrate with another, because when something is dualistic in nature even its subtlest form remains dualistic. Science has analyzed matter down to its tiniest particles, but even particles at their most fundamental level are still mutually exclusive. Some people might feel they have a very good understanding of who they are and exclaim, "This is who I am!!" However, such thinking is merely an extension of the false concept of self.

Buddhism, science and medical research are unable to find an unchanging, substantial entity that can be identified as the "I." The formation of this concept—of an unchanging, substantial "I"—is due to the inertia caused by habitually grasping at phenomena. It is a tendency that has been cultivated over time through unconscious attachment to phenomena in every moment of mental functioning. Each thought arising from the mind continually grasps at phenomena, solidifying the strength of this unconscious grasping until it gives rise to a false sense of independent existence. Using this false core as the self to interact with situations brings forth a fixed pattern of thinking and a rigid set of personality traits. This false, independent core and its rigid ways of mind functioning become the so-called "I."

Accordingly, "I" is for most people merely a falsehood. It is a constantly changing, compounded, passive and fabricated "I." It is not the pure essence that is the Source of Life, nor is it the Pure

Mind, meaning the True Self. A poem by Shao-Jung goes like this: *"The 'I' of yesterday is the 'you' of today; the 'I' of today knows not to whom it shall belong."*

Venerable Cao-Tang also said, *"A performer is just one body, sometimes an official but sometimes the servant; though his name and clothing may change, ultimately there is no distinction between the master and the servant."* The Pure Mind accomplishes all functions, and everything is inseparable from the Mind. The Pure Mind is the True Self; this Mind is formless but is able to function, containing all experiences, functions and phenomena.

The minds of the saints are like sponges that absorb and exude immediately. Always empty and clean, they are free of residual fluid. The mind of an ordinary person, however, is like a sponge that soaks up and holds on to many different fluids, the residual patterning of self-centered functioning determined by an infinite possibility of information input and experiences. The content of this sponge is simply the habitual tendency: the unconscious functioning pattern of the false self, which in turn is merely a composition of past experiences and ideas. The individual adopts his habitual patterns as his personality, surrounding himself with deluded thoughts and taking them to be "my thoughts," which he then uses to define and recognize the so-called "I."

The so-called "I" is nothing other than habitual thinking. Anything outside the scope of an individual's self-created habitual thinking is not considered "I." The existence of "I" in man's consciousness is simply a habitual delusion, not the truth. Such "I" is only the functional composition of habitual thinking, lacking a substantive core. Man can always change himself, just as the fluid in a sponge can be squeezed out in order for other kinds of liquids to be absorbed.

Although ordinary beings have already filled themselves with ideas that define their "I," and have grown used to certain lifestyles and modes of perception, they can still clear away false views through spiritual practice that stops their unconscious mode of functioning. To accomplish the realization of the nature of the Mind, they must practice according to the correct teaching and right views. Such teaching and views are inseparable from emptiness-awareness, which is the essential nature of the Mind.

One of the most precious sutras of Mahayana Buddhism is the *Diamond Sutra*, formally called *"Diamond Prajna Paramita."* The direct translation of *Prajna* is "great wisdom," or the wisdom that transcends dualism. The wisdom of the Pure Mind is like a flawless diamond: clear, perfect and indestructible. Due to their indestructible hardness, diamonds are used to cut and polish various objects. The *Diamond Sutra* takes the meaning of the word "diamond" in the sense of the perfection, omnipotence, eternity and indestructibility of the wisdom manifested from the Mind in a state of purity. The Light of Wisdom can penetrate and sever the false I-consciousness and dissolve all worldly vexations, attachments and habitual tendencies. *Paramita* is a Sanskrit term for "reaching the other shore": It means leaving this shore of ignorance, confusion and dualistic confrontations, and arriving at the other shore of awakening, clarity and serenity.

*Prajna Paramita* therefore means "great wisdom reaching the other shore," thus representing the manifestation of the pure, formless, diamond-like wisdom of the Mind. *Prajna* also represents the Mind's non-dualistic luminosity, which is free of delusion and attachment. It is the absolutely pure, non-dualistic wisdom, or the essence of the Pure Mind. Although the Mind is formless, it manifests and is cognizant of the source of all existence.

Dualism creates the mutually dependent existence of time and space. A dualistic world can never transcend the boundary and limits of time and space. Any mental conception that includes the idea of time and space cannot transcend duality, either. The Mind is emptiness, which encompasses all existence and manifests all phenomena through its functioning.

Only through the withdrawal of all phenomena into the Mind itself—using it as the reference point for all functioning and all phenomena—is it possible to reach beyond the dualistic distinction. Time is created by the apparent variation in the order in which unconsciously arising thoughts appear, and space is the result of various conditional factors in the presence of thoughts. Different thoughts lead to different time and space. Because man merely recognizes thoughts but not the essence of the Mind behind the thoughts, he grasps thoughts as the self and succumbs to the illusion of time and space.

Here is a story that demonstrates how time and space are creations of the Mind and explains the emptiness, formlessness and all-pervasiveness of the Mind's functioning:

National Teacher Hui-Chung, of the Tang Dynasty, was a disciple of the Sixth Patriarch Hui-Neng and attained enlightenment under his guidance. After awakening to the Way, he went into retreat in the

Dan-Tzi Valley of White Cliff Mountain for forty years. Emperor Xu Zung knew of his attainment and invited him to be the national teacher.

One day, the Indian Tripitaka master called Great Ear, who was well known for his ability as a mind reader, came to visit the Xu Zung. The Emperor decided to test the attainment of the visitor by comparing his wisdom and spiritual power to those of the national teacher. The Emperor arranged a meeting.

The two men met, whereupon Hui-Chung asked Great Ear: "Do you have mind-reading power?"

Great Ear affirmed politely, "Dare not!"

Hui-Chung said, "Tell me where this old monk is right now."

"While being the honorable teacher of a nation, why have you gone to the West River to watch the boat races?" responded Great Ear.

After a while, Hui-Chung said again, "Tell me where this old monk is right now."

"Venerable, you are the teacher of a nation, why have you gone to watch the monkeys' play on the Tien-Jing bridge?"

For the third time Hui-Chung said, "Tell me where this old monk is." Great Ear exhausted all his energy trying to search the teacher's thoughts, but he found no trace. The teacher exhorted him, "Wild fox! Tell me, where is this mind-reading ability of yours!?" Great Ear was dumbfounded.

National Teacher Hui-Chung possessed great wisdom. In that moment, he had withdrawn all thoughts into emptiness and manifested the emptiness and tranquility of the Pure Mind. Great

Ear was unable to read any thoughts because Hui-Chung's mind was resting calmly in the formless awareness of true emptiness. In the dharma realm of true emptiness, no one could find him, not even the Buddha. This is how National Teacher Hui-Chung dispatched Great Ear, and the emperor rejoiced, having proved the wisdom of inviting Hui-Chung to serve as a teacher.

Each thought is a universe. Where the thought is, life is already unfolding. However, ordinary beings are obsessed with the physical body of the present and the karmic reality. They are unable to recognize that each thought spreading over the worlds of the ten directions is the true home of life in each moment. Therefore, to make the most authentic life of the present moment we must live in the present moment and restrain the prejudiced delusion that breaks reality into pieces. All forms of existence are the creation of the Mind's different functioning, like the many brilliant facets of a flawless diamond. If we can always manifest the present moment, live in the present moment, function from the essence of the Mind and remain aware of the Mind's functioning while abiding in the essential ground of the Mind, then we can transcend time and space.

The transcendence of time and space is the end of reincarnation. Without this attachment, we are no longer hindered by object and phenomena, because the appearance and disappearance of phenomena occur simultaneously. Nothing is permanent, so not even the reflection of a flawless diamond can be retained. Similarly, the mirror can reflect any image but no image can be captured. When we are able to function while abiding in the pure, diamond-like Mind, we will not go through the rounds of reincarnation again. As in the story of National Teacher Hui-Chung, when we live in the present moment with the lucid and aware emptiness of the diamond-like Mind, we become our own master in each moment, leaving no trace anywhere.

In the moment of his enlightenment, Zen Master Xianyan uttered the following verse:

*One strike, all knowledge is forgotten,*
*No artificial cultivation is necessary after all,*
*Every moment I uphold the ancient Way,*
*Never retreating into silent stagnation,*
*Nowhere shall I leave any trace,*
*Virtue that is beyond sound and form,*
*Everywhere those who attained the Way,*
*All declare this to be the highest order.*

To find your own inner diamond treasure, you must recognize that you are no longer the passive product of thoughts arising from the Mind. You are the Mind, and you have the ability to give rise to thoughts and functions. You have the ability to change the course of your life and fulfill your true aspiration.

Spiritual practice is similar to the process of decorating your home. Not only is it possible for you to redecorate as an individual, it is also possible for mankind to change the inner environment of his home, his real home, the home of all phenomena, which is the Mind. Do not become so stubborn in thinking, "This is how I am!" Such a belief is not the truth but merely an illusory extension of your false self. The habit of holding onto thoughts such as, "This is how I am!" or "This is the way I deal with people!" prevents you from living your life in honest terms. When decorating your home, if there is a large sofa blocking the hallway, it is obvious you should remove it.

If your life has not turned out according to your expectations, it is time to recognize and face the issue so that you can find a solution. Start with seeing the fault in your behaviors and reactions, and then practice changing them by changing your thoughts. Cultivate the ability to focus the mind and redirect your thoughts under quiet conditions. Polish the mind's awareness in the activities of your daily life so that, one by one, the vexations and obstacles in your life can gradually be dissolved. Endeavor to de-construct the false concept of "I" and train yourself to change the habits associated with it. Once you rid your mind of these defilements, you can rest at ease in the Pure Mind, comfortably abiding in the unborn, undestroyed, eternal emptiness and luminosity of Life.

## Worldly Phenomena Thus Go

Always remember that the Mind is formless; that it is emptiness, ever aware and luminous. The Mind exists just as it is, and is manifested just as it is. While in essence it has no form, it is able to respond as an object and manifest forms, because it is all-pervasive in the phenomenal world. There is no limit to the thoughts the Mind can generate. Therefore, when you use the Mind skillfully, according to its nature as emptiness, you can break down what is and replace it with what is correct.

The Mind has infinite malleability and potential, so in one

instant a thought can change, planting a new concept and renewing the self. The self can be changed because it has no real root; it is not an unchanging, substantial entity. Not even the subtlest, most ingrained self-attachment or habitual tendency has a substantiated existence. Nor can you create a thread of life evolution that connects the various roles and forms of existences in any way that makes sense out of such habitual tendencies.

Attachment makes it difficult to change the mind. When you mistake the false, baseless thoughts as "I," with the illusion that there is something to gain or something to be possessed—thereby overlaying falsehood upon falsehood—you create your own prison. As long as the false I-consciousness remains, you will never enjoy true freedom and liberation. Instead, you will continually intertwine the difficulties and suffering created by your self-attachment.

Be diligent in removing the erroneous beliefs and illusions, recognize your true self and the innate, authentic Mind, and you will finally actualize the wholeness of emptiness, awareness and luminosity. The True Mind has no inner-outer distinction; there is neither "I" nor "others"; there is no relativity, because it is beyond duality. The entire universe, which includes your mind and body, is the manifestation of the True Mind. Thus it is said that the mountains, rivers and the great earth are the complete display of the body of the King of Dharma. The True Mind is the Collective and the Creator, the essence of which is the universal truth.

The defiled mind of an ordinary being is like a mirror smeared with paint: The mirror loses the clarity of its reflection, while the man mistakes the colored paint on the mirror as his true self. This is a stubborn delusion and a severe distortion of reality. What is fortunate in all this is that the essence of the Mind is emptiness, awareness and luminosity. Regardless of how the Pure Mind has been contaminated, this pure nature is forever present in all times and seasons. You can always replace your old ideas and concepts, break through your attachments, and attain enlightenment and liberation. Through the accumulation of merit and wisdom, your bodhisattva aspiration shall be fulfilled and the state of Buddhahood shall be attained.

Life will be full of contradictions and conflicts until you become the master of your mind and your self. Man unconsciously manufactures misconceptions about reality. Having an erroneous belief in his identity and how he can affect his own future, he lives a life of confusion and misperception. To become your own master, you must first clearly recognize the Mind and realize that all existences are manifestations of the Mind. The essence of the Mind surpasses the contradictions of duality. It is the false identification with your attachment that creates your troubles and suffering. It is the grasping of your own mind's function that unnecessarily confines the Mind, which is otherwise unlimited, infinitely capable and omniscient.

Familiarize yourself with the concepts in this book, and you will find that life can turn around completely. Apply what you have learned, and begin the process of letting go of your false ideas and way of life in order to become the master of your mind and your life. You are more than just your thoughts, you are the person who gives rise to thoughts. Therefore, give rise to thoughts from your True

Self, and let the selfless nature of the Pure Mind subdue the ordinary tendencies of the mind. It is taught in the sutra that a bodhisattva shall "*abide as is, subdue the mind as is.*"

Master Da-An paid a visit to master Bai-Zhang and asked, "For a practitioner who seeks to know the Buddha, what is it?"

Master Bai-Zhang answered, "Much like seeking the cow while riding the cow." What he meant is that his questioning was similar to looking for the cow while riding it. The mind that is questioning right now is the answer itself, so using that mind to find another mind is futile.

Da-An then asked, "After seeing the cow, then what?" In other words, once the Mind is found and the essential nature is recognized, what should you do about it?

Bai-Zhang replied, "Just like man riding the cow home." By realizing the Way, having broken the attachment, you can return to your true home.

Da-An followed with another question: "From the beginning to the end, how should one maintain the practice?" Even when you have returned home, how can you stay, abiding in your true home?

Bai-Zhang instructed, "Like a cow herder, discipline it with the staff of vigilance so it does not trample the crops."

Just as the cow herder will take a whip to the cow when it wanders or goes out of control, continue to discipline the mind. This is the hands-on approach to practice. The ancients said, "*Step by step, one tread on solid ground.*" Do not allow your mind to drift with the flow of phenomena, but instead keep every thought inseparable from awareness, inseparable from the Mind, and abide as is.

Zen Master Wu-Men, of the Sung dynasty, wrote a poem: "*Spring flowers and autumn moon, summer breeze and winter snow, as long as no distraction hangs in the mind, it is the perfect season of life.*" To a mind free of obstructions, every day is a great day; the Mind's functioning pervades the great space, and the essence of the Mind is undefiled by dust. With diseased eyes, myriad illusions will manifest like a shower of flowers from the sky, but without disease everything is clear and lucid. Unrestricted, the Mind's vast capacity is boundless. Through Zen training and the transformation of thought creation, through the deconstruction of the false self and its functioning, attachment and contamination, the true nature of the Mind shall gradually emerge.

The ancients said, "*Practice takes a man with the strength of steel, in order to discern the Source within the Mind. Going directly for the attainment of unsurpassed awakening, putting down all distractions of right and wrong.*" Putting the teaching in real practice, all wisdom will manifest as a result of the eradication of attachments. After you realize the Source, you will diligently cultivate the Way.

Zen Master Shiang-An described his experience of cultivation after realizing the Way: "*Last year I was poor, but not yet in poverty; this year, I am poor, the beginning of true poverty. Last year I was poor, but there was still a spot for an awl to stand; this year, there is not even an awl.*" The cessation of the mind of the Three Realms is the unborn, undestroyed nirvana, arousing great compassion from this unborn, undestroyed Mind to awaken oneself and others and establish all beings in the Buddha's Way. This is the actualization of the highest freedom: liberation, wisdom, compassion, fulfillment and eternity.

*"There is nothing special to cultivate in practice, only a matter of recognizing the Path; upon recognizing the Path, birth and death shall cease together."* The Pure Mind is the refuge of withdrawal for all vexations and delusions; the sole destination of spiritual practice, the ultimate actualization of eternal life. The sutra said, *"The principle may be realized suddenly, all confusions dispelled simultaneously; but phenomena cannot be eliminated at once, instead only to be exhausted in stages."* Now that you are in possession of everything you need to make a change, it is up to you to make a diligent effort one step at a time. Freedom and perfect ease come from constant cultivation, but of course, in the ultimate sense it is redundant to talk about cultivation:

The Awakened Self Nature,

Primordially pure it is.

Just use this Mind,

Directly actualize Buddhahood.

The Patriarch's Ox,

Led to the Home's door;

Squandering time asking how,

In the blink of an eye, the King of Hell detains.

Utter a phrase that strikes thunderous in the sky,

Take a step that shakes the earth alight;

I have not mystical power nor marvelous feat,

It is just a magnificent technology.

# GLOSSARY

# GLOSSARY

AGAMA SUTRA: The *Agama Sutra* is a collection of early texts of Buddhism.

AMIDA BUDDHA: The Amida Buddha is the root teacher of the Western Land of Bliss.

VENERABLE ANANDA: Venerable Ananda is the Buddha's cousin and his attendant. Among the ten chief disciples of the Buddha, Ananda is known for having attended the most teachings and for his remarkable memory of the spoken words of the Buddha. He is well respected and remembered for his gentle nature, eagerness to be of help, and great empathy with other's suffering. He often requests teachings from the Buddha on behalf of others, and is instrumental in the establishment of the order of nuns. Venerable Ananda is also the third patriarch of Zen, starting with the historical Buddha himself.

ARAHANT: An arahant is one who has attained a spiritual state of liberation where habitual tendencies, such as defining and clinging to the notion of 'I', have been purified to the point that the individual is free from life after life of reincarnation.

ARAHANTSHIP: Arahantship is the spiritual state in which an arahant dwells.

ATTACHMENT: Attachment is a state of mind characterized by grasping or holding onto mental functions, such as thoughts, feelings, and perceptions. The most fundamental attachment human beings have is to their sense of an independent selfhood.

AVALOKITESHVARA: The Bodhisattva of Compassion, also known as Chenrezig in Tibetan, or Kwan-Yin in Chinese is Avalokiteshvara. As a central figure in Mahayana Buddhism, Avalokiteshvara is the embodiment of great compassion that arises from the profound understanding of the true nature of reality. Avalokiteshvara also represents the compassion that arises as a pure function of the Mind.

MASTER BAI-YUN SHO-DUAN (ALSO WHITE CLOUD ZEN MASTER) (1025–72): Master Bai-Yun is of the Lin-Ji lineage; the forty-sixth generation in Zen from the historical Buddha. One day his teacher Master Yang-Qi asked whether he remembered the poem of enlightenment of his master of ordination.

Bai-Yun said he remembered and recited it: "I possess a lustrous pearl/locked and concealed by dust and burden/now that the dust is clear away and the light shines through/illuminating the ten thousand mountains and rivers." Upon hearing this, Master Yang-Qi, jumped up and laughed out loud. Bai-Yun was dumbfounded and could not sleep for the whole night. Next day Master Yang-Qi asked, "Did you witness the exorcism yesterday?" (This conversation occurs during the time of year where there are staged dramas among the lay people for the purpose of expelling evil spirits.) Bai-Yun said, "Yes." Yang-Qi said, "You can't match up to it." Bai-Yun asked, "What do you mean?" Yang-Qi said, "It loves people's laughter, while you fear people's laughter." Upon hearing this, Master Bai-Yun attained enlightenment.

MASTER BAI-ZHANG: Master Bai-Zhang Huai-Hai (720–814) is the teacher of Huang-Bo and instrumental in reforming and establishing the rules that governed how Zen practitioners should live and practice together as a self-sustaining community where in addition to meditation, manual labor for farming and up-keeping of the monastery became an integral part of Zen practice. The event that is the precursor to his enlightenment went like this: One time he was attending to Master Ma-tzu and a flock of wild geese flew by. Ma-tzu asked him, "What is it?" Bai-zhang replied, "Wild geese." Ma-tzu then asked, "Where did it go?" Bai-zhang said, "They flew away." Without warning, Ma-tzu turned around and got a hold of Bai-zhang's nose and twisted hard. Bai-zhang cried out in pain, and Ma-tzu said, "And you told me it flew away?!" At this instant, Bai-zhang had some realization. Returning to his quarter, Bai-zhang began crying and a fellow monk asked him, "Are you missing your folks?" "No." "Did you get scolded by the teacher?" "No." "Then why are you crying?" Bai-zhang said, "My nose was twisted by master and the pain didn't quite penetrate through!" The other monk then asked, "What is not working out?" Bai-zhang said, "Go ask the master himself." When the monk asked the master about the situation, Ma-tzu said, "He [Bai-zhang] knows it, go ask him!" When the monk returned, Bai-zhang was laughing out loud! Puzzled, he said, "Bai-zhang, you were just crying, how come you are now laughing so hard?" Bai-zhang said, "Was just crying, now laughing." The monk was still puzzled. Later on Bai-zhang achieved further break through and his realization was confirmed by Ma-tzu.

BODHI TREE: The Bodhi Tree is the sacred fig tree in Bodh Gaya, India, under which the historical Buddha attained enlightenment. Bodhi is a Sanskrit term meaning "awakening."

BODHIDHARMA: Believed to have died sometime near 536 AD, *Bodhidharma* is considered the First Patriarch of Zen in China and the twenty-eighth embodiment of enlightenment since the historical Buddha. An Indian monk, Bodhidharma traveled to China to spread the teaching by focusing on the essence of dharma and freeing people from the traps of religious dogmatism. He meditated for nine years in seclusion, facing the wall in a cave near the Shao-Lin temple (often regarded as the birthplace of kung-fu) until he met Hui-Ke, who attained realization of the truth through Bodhidharma's instruction and became the second Zen patriarch. In Zen, the transmission of the teaching is made directly from mind to mind; the disciple's realization is verified not by intellectual judgment or understanding, but by confirmation through the teacher's intuitive evaluation. Since the essence of the dharma is beyond intellectual reasoning, only those who have directly realized the truth may assess and confirm the attainment of a student. The analogy often given is that only a person who has drunk the water truly knows its taste; only the teacher is able to assess whether a student has also tasted the elixir of the true dharma. The tradition of the Zen lineage in China starts with Bodhidharma's transmission to Hui-Ke and continues to the Sixth Patriarch Hui-Neng whose revolutionizing of the Zen teaching lead to the eventual creation of the five schools of Zen Buddhism. One of several recorded teaching attributed to Bodhidharma is the Treatise on the Two Entrances and Four Practices, a short teaching that described two approaches and four practice methods that lead to spiritual realization.

BODHISATTVA: A *bodhisattva* is a practitioner—either in the process of attaining or having already attained a high-level of spiritual awakening and freedom from suffering—who strives to help others to achieve the same state. This altruistic action is based on the profound recognition of the inseparability of the personal self and others. The term *bodhisattva* also represents the myriad pure functions that arise from the Pure Mind.

BUDDHAHOOD: Buddhahood is the spiritual state of complete liberation from suffering and perfection of all virtues. It is the state of complete realization of the essence of the Mind and the perfection of the Mind's functions.

CONFUCIANISM: A set of ethical doctrines preached by Confucius (551–478 BCE) that has been highly influential in China. Confucianism stresses the importance of proper conduct and responsibilities in the context of relationships, such as the relationship between rulers and the ruled, father and son, husband and wife, elders and the young, and between friends. It is a humanistic ethical system not based on any theistic belief.

CHAO-CHOU ("JOSHU" IN JAPANESE): One of the most famous Chinese Zen Masters in the Tang Dynasty (618-907 AD), Chao-Chou is widely known for the classic *koan* where in response to the question of whether a dog possesses the Buddha Nature—the potential for awakening—he uttered the word 'Wu' (or 'Mu' in Japanese) that is often incorporated into the practice of Zen inquiry.

CHI-KUNG: *Chi-Kung* is a Chinese term meaning "vital energy cultivation." It is a broad category of techniques ranging from silent meditation to physical exercises of varying degree of intensity. The Chinese believe that the cultivation of *chi*—a subtle form of energy in the physical body—is vital to health and a balanced mind.

MASTER DA-AN: Master Da-An (?-883) took monastic vow in Huang-Bo mountain and studied several years the monastic code of discipline. Yearning for the highest teaching, he left and met Master Bai-zhang and attained enlightenment. He once addressed an assembly of monks, "Since you are all here, just settle down. What is there to seek? If you seek to be the Buddha, you are already the Buddha! Why keep wandering around other's house, restless like a thirsty deer under a scorching sun! How can you ever find what you seek this way?"

MASTER DA-HUI: Master Da-Hui (1089-1163) is the most well-known advocate of the Huatou practice—the continuous and intensive questioning of a koan as crystallized by a single phrase or a single word such as "Wu" (or Mu in Japanese) or "What is the meaning of Bodhidharma's coming from the West?" or "Who is the one reciting the Buddha's Name?" The purpose of the Huatou practice is to utilize the doubt generated by the questioning to penetrate through our habitual attachments and to directly experience the nature of the pure mind.

DHARMA: *Dharma* literally means law, rule, or duty. It may refer to the Buddhist teaching or to the ultimate truth being expressed by the teaching. In Buddhist philosophy, the term dharma is also used to refer to phenomenon.

DHARMAKAYA: *Dharmakaya*, literally "Truth Body" in Sanskrit, constitutes the primordial essence of the Mind out of which all phenomena arise.

DIAMOND SUTRA: A Mahayana Sutra, based on a dialogue between the Buddha and his disciple Subhuti, which focuses on the practice of overcoming dualism and attachment to forms.

DZOGCHEN: The Dzogchen philosophy of Tibetan Buddhism, meaning "Great Perfection," teaches that since enlightenment is already here in the present moment, practice is solely for the purpose of recognizing this truth.

EMPTINESS: The word "Emptiness" refers to the lack of intrinsic existence of any phenomena.

MASTER FA-RONG (594–657): Master Fa-Rong was a disciple of the Fourth Patriarch Dao-Xin. According to the story, Fa-Rong read the Nirvana Sutra and realized the path he wanted to take for the rest of his life, therefore he lived and practiced in seclusion in the mountain. When Fourth Patriarch Dao-Xin found Fa-Rong, he was sitting quietly in meditation. The Fourth Patriarch then asked him, "what are you doing?" Fa-Rong said, "watching the mind." Dao-Xin then asked him, "Tell me then, what is it that is watching the mind? And what is the mind?" Fa-Rong was unable to respond and went on to receive instruction from the Fourth Patriarch.

FANG-TZUEN DISCOURSE: Written by the fourth patriarch of Zen, the Fang-Tzuen Discourse points out that the root of everything is the Mind. All reality—physical and mental—is nothing but the mind; all forms of practice are nothing but cultivation of the mind. The term "fang-tzuen" in Chinese means a small area about the size of our palm or our heart. The term is also used as a metaphor for the mind.

FIVE AGGREGATES: The Five Aggregates are the five aspects that comprise our experiential reality: matter (or form), feeling, perception, volition (or mental constructs), and consciousness.

FOUR ELEMENTS: The Four Elements are Earth, Water, Fire and Wind, but more precisely, these refer to the qualities of solidity, fluidity, heat and motion possessed by material phenomena.

FOUR NOBLE TRUTHS: The first sermon taught by the historical Buddha, the Four Noble Truths are: (1) the nature of suffering, (2) the cause of suffering is attachment, (3) suffering ceases when attachment is removed, and (4) the way to remove attachment is through proper cultivation of eight aspects of our life: understanding (or view) of reality, thought, speech, action, livelihood, effort, attention, and mental concentration.

FOURTH PATRIARCH OF ZEN: Zen patriarchs are considered the orthodox line of transmission of Zen teaching, the embodiment of the direct realization of the truth rather than mere intellectual understanding or written words. The fourth patriarch in China recognized as having attained this direct realization of the truth was Daoxin (580–651 AD).

GOLDEN OX: A Zen master famous for laughing while calling the monks to take their meal. Others Zen masters in the past who also deployed unusual means of teaching include Chao-Chou (Joshu), who is known for his tea offering to visiting practitioners; Yun-Men Master, known for his cake; and Lin-Ji Master who uses a sudden shout to affect a break-through in the student's realization.

HUA-YEN: In Chinese *Hua-Yen* means Flower Garlands. A school of Buddhism emerged in the sixth century in China based on the teaching of the Flower Garland

MASTER HUANG-BO: Zen Master Huang-Bo (or Huang-Po) (776–856) is the teacher of Master Lin-Ji, widely known for his directness in pointing out the One Mind, beyond language and form. Huang-Bo is the name of the mountain where he taught. It is customary in China to refer to a Zen master by his place of residence. Teaching on the emptiness of the mind, he said: "Ordinary beings focus on situation, but the practitioners of the Way focus on the mind; to forget both mind and situation is the real dharma. To forget the situation is relatively easy, in comparison to the utmost difficult task of forgetting the mind. Men are afraid to forget the mind because they fear the emptiness, where there is nothing to hold on; he did not realize that true emptiness is not nothingness, it is simply the realm of One Truth."

MASTER HUNG-CHIH CHENG-CHUEH (OR HONGZHI ZHENGUE) (1091–1157): A key figure in the Caodong lineage of Zen. Master Hung-Chih Cheng-Chueh pioneered the practice of silent illumination—the precursor to the practice of Zazen ("Just Sitting") that is very popular in Japan. He is also known as Tian-Tong, which is the name of his resident monastery. Dogen, the founder of Rinzai Zen in Japan, studied in Tian-Tong monastery in China before returning to Japan.

KARMA: Karma means action. It also refers to the result of action, since the spiritual law of cause and effect states that result is always preceded by causal action. Karma is sometimes misunderstood as a kind of fatalism, but, the ultimate cause of all phenomena is the Mind, so mastery of the Mind provides mastery of karma.

KOAN: A koan is literally a "public case," a record of Zen dialogue. These dialogues are often used as means to test a student's realization. These dialogues can seem absurd, illogical or trivial and can generate a sense of bewilderment or doubt in the student's mind which can only be resolved by transcending conventional thought and attachment.

LAYMAN FU: Fu Shan-Hui (497–569), a contemporary of Bodhidharma, was highly regarded for his spiritual attainment. His Mind-King is a classic writing for Zen study. In Buddhism, many examples of lay practitioners who have exceptionally high spiritual attainment exist. Another famous example is Vimalakirti, a layman whose teaching to the chief disciples of the Buddha and many bodhisattvas are recorded in the Vimalakirti Nirdesa Sutra. This respect for lay practitioners demonstrates the essential idea in Buddhism that all beings possess the Buddha Nature, the potential for awakening. Regardless of external form, the essence of all beings and the Buddhas is the same.

MASTER LIN-JI: Zen Master Lin-Ji (787–867) is the founder of the Lin-Ji school of Zen, five generations after the Sixth Patriarch Hui-Neng. Lin-Ji approached his teacher, Master Huang-Bo, three times to ask for the true meaning of Buddha dharma. Each time before he could even finish his sentence, he was hit by Huang-Bo. Discouraged, he took leave and went to Master Da-Yu and related his encounter. Da-Yu told him that Huang-Bo did it out of of his motherly heart of kindness. Upon hearing this Lin-Ji attained awakening and commented that Huang-Bo's teaching is not so great! Well-known for rigorous and intensive teaching style, Master Lin-Ji utilized the so-called 'four shouts' and 'eight staffs' as means for breaking student's attachment, no doubt due to the influence of his own awakening experience.

LIN-JI SCHOOL OF ZEN: Also known as Rinzai in Japanese, Lin-Ji is one of the five schools of Zen that originated in ancient China and is most representative of Zen practice today. The Lin-Ji school of Zen, founded by Master Lin-Ji (d. 867), is characterized by its intensity of practice and the use of a 'shout' or a 'staff' as a means of lighting the spark of realization in the practitioner. Today only the Lin-Ji school and Caodong (or "Soto" in Japanese) school of Zen still remain.

MAHAMUDRA: Mahamudra, "Great Seal," is a school of Tibetan Buddhism. This name implies that all existence is sealed with the essence of the absolute.

MAHAYANA: Mahayana, one of the major schools Buddhism, literally means "great vehicle." Central to the Mahayana teaching is the concept of the bodhisattva, for whom altruism is a key aspect of the spiritual path, being motivated by selfless compassion arising from the realization of the essential inseparability between himself and others. While other schools of Buddhism may not emphasize the ideal of a bodhisattva path, it should be recognized that each path manifests according to the karma of the individual practitioner, just as different illness requires unique medicine to affect a cure. Practices that seem focused on liberating the practicioner's own suffering can also contribute significantly to the well-being of others. The merit of any path should only be judged within the context of the practitioner's unique situation in terms of its suitability to guide that individual toward the realization of the universal truth.

MAITREYA: Maitreya is the next Buddha who will appear in our world. In Zen, Maitreya represents the Mind's pure function in the present moment.

MANDALA: A visualization of the universe, a mandala is an idealized environment that symbolizes the manifestation of the Pure Mind.

MANTRA: A sacred sound, either one syllable in a word or a set of words that have spiritual or mystical power, a mantra may have power to protect, purify, eliminate, or magnify certain states of consciousness as well as generating other effects. The power of a mantra comes from the pure function of the Mind, which is evoked by the repetition of the mantra.

MEIJI: A period of Japanese modernization from 1868 to 1912, during the rule of Meiji Emperor.

MERIT: Merit is often considered to be the "positive force" that leads to desirable results in our life experience. More precisely, merit is the difference in the reality manifested by the Mind due to an elevated spiritual state of attainment.

MIND DHARMA: Mind *dharma* is the aspect of Buddhist teachings that directly address the nature of the Mind.

MIND GROUND: The Mind can be described in terms of its essence, form, and functions. Mind Ground refers to the essence aspect of the Mind.

MIND KING: Since all functions of the mind—such as perception, feeling, and consciousness—arise from the Mind, this Mind is regarded as the "king," the governing essence of all functions. The term "Mind King" appeared in a hymn written by the third patriarch Seng-Ts'an, who lived in the sixth century AD. It is also the name of a hymn, attributed to Layman Fu, which is a classic in Zen study.

MASTER NAN-YUE HUI-RANG: Master Nan-yue Hui-rang (677–744) is one of the two main disciples of the Sixth Patriarch Hui-Neng. The Lin-Ji and Gui-Yang schools of Zen emerged from the lineage of Nan-yue Hui-rang; whereas the Cao-Dong, Fa-Yen, and Yun-Men schools arise through the Sixth Patriarch's other main disciple Qing-Yuan Xing-Si.

NIRMANAKAYA: The moment-to-moment manifestation of phenomena from the Mind, *nirmanakaya* is often used to refer specifically to the manifestation of the Buddha's physical presence from the essence of the Mind.

NIRVANA: *Nirvana* is an eternal state of liberation, where the suffering of cyclic birth and death ends both on the gross level of the physical body, or on the subtle level of moment-to-moment manifestation and disappearance of phenomena. Liberation from birth and death does not negate the nature of phenomena. Rather, it frees the practitioner from attachment to phenomena as something permanent so that the changing nature of phenomena no longer causes fundamental struggle or suffering within him.

PARINIRVANA: The state of nirvana upon the death of the physical body of an enlightened being is often referred to as parinirvana. It symbolizes the complete purification of all traces of impure karma. Alternatively, parinirvana can be understood to be a state of liberation where the function of the Mind has been completely purified.

PLATFORM SUTRA: The Platform Sutra contains a recorded biography and account of the life and teaching of the Sixth Patriarch of Zen, Hui-Neng. The title of this book is based on the opening verse of this sutra: The Awakened Self Nature,/ Primordially pure it is./Just use this Mind,/Directly actualize Buddhahood.

This sutra contains the wisdom and essence of early Zen teaching in China. When it was written, its highly accessible language pointed out the formless truth that underlies all existence, dispelled many common misunderstandings of classical scripture, and revealed the true purpose behind various forms of popular religious practices. Through time, this sutra has remained highly relevant to modern society as spiritual seekers attempt to cut through various presentations to discover the real message.

POET BAI (OR LI BAI): Li Bai (701–762) is considered one of the greatest poets in Chinese history. His poetry is characterized by its spontaneity and influence of Taoism and Zen. He was also referred to as the Poet Transcendent or the Retired Scholar of Azure Lotus. One of his most famous poems is called the "Drinking along under Moonlight" and has been translated into English.

POWA: Powa is a Tibetan practice for transferring of a practicioner's conscious-ness at the time of death in order to cause a favorable rebirth.

PURE LAND: The pure living environment manifested by a Buddha through the pure function of the Mind is the pure land. The power of his vows makes each Buddha's pure land unique in its characteristics and the manifestation of an idealized environment for facilitating his own spiritual practice. Practitioners of pure land Buddhism purify their minds and vow to take rebirth after death in the Buddha's pure land in order to further his spiritual practice. Since the mind and our physical environment are inseparable aspects of the same essence, the practice of pure land is essentially the practice of purifying the mind.

REALM OF FLOWER ADORNMENT: (or Flower Garland, See Hua-Yen)

SAKYAMUNI: Sakya (or Shakya) is the Buddha's clan of origin in northern India, near the foothill of the Himalayas in present day Nepal. The historical Buddha, known as Sakyamuni ("Sage of the Sakya") Buddha (563–483 BCE), was born a prince. He abandoned a life of wealth, power, and luxury in order to pursue a spiritual journey on which he sought to resolve the problems of inevitable suffering of birth, death, illness, and aging that he observed when venturing outside the protective environment of his palace.

**SAMANTABHADRA:** The bodhisattva that symbolizes spiritual vows and action is Samantabhadra. In Mahayana Buddhism, wisdom and action are two critical aspects of spiritual practice that must be cultivated together. Without action, true wisdom cannot arise since intellectual reasoning alone cannot grasp the profound teaching. However, without wisdom and right understanding to guide his action, a practitioner may fall into delusion and the cycle of karmic suffering.

**SAMBOGHAKYA:** *Samboghakya* is the pure primordial awareness of the Mind.

**SAMSARA:** The cycles of birth, death and rebirth in the world of appearance are referred to as *samsara*. In Buddhist cosmology, *samsara* is typically described as six different states of existence determined by a person's accumulated habitual tendencies and dominant *karma*. In brief, these six realms are: heavenly being, human, jealous god, hungry ghost, animal and hell being.

Rebirth as a heavenly being is due to a predominance of compassion, loving-kindness, sympathetic joy, and equanimity in consciousness and actions. Being reborn as a jealous god occurs due to causes such as charitable actions conducted with regret or impure motivation that lead to material abundance but strongly felt sense of dissatisfaction and jealousy. Existence as a human being is the result of mixed positive and negative thought, speech, and action, none of which is very strong. The hungry ghost state is characterized by greed and craving; the animal realm is dominated by a lack of awareness and delusion; and reincarnation as a hell being is caused by negative afflictions, such as anger or actions (such as killing) carried out with strong intent and accumulated forces.

*Samsara* can also be understood as a metaphor of our moment-to-moment state of consciousness. The moment a person gives rise to compassion in the mind, that individual is manifesting the heavenly being's existence on Earth. The very next moment, the arising of greed can manifest the mode of being of a hungry ghost. From this perspective, rebirth in a different realm does not just occur after physical death, but is instead the process of the moment-to-moment manifestation of the mind's function.

**SANGHA:** The *sangha* often refers to the monastic community, but it also includes the community of all Buddhist practitioners, both lay and monastic. The sangha is significant because without those who actually practice, teach, and embody the wisdom and compassion of the teaching in their daily life, the real benefit and goal of the teaching cannot be fulfilled.

SEAL OF DHARMA: The seal of the *dharma* refers to the characteristics of phenomenon: impermanence, non-self, and suffering. Sometimes a fourth aspect is added which states that *nirvana* is true peace. *Nirvana* refers to the essence of all existence that is beyond conditionality and not subject to birth and death.

SENG-ZHAO: A prominent Chinese Buddhist monk who lived between 374 and 414. He is a disciple of Kumarajiva, a scholar Buddhist monk from Kucha, who translated many Indian Buddhist texts to Chinese. Seng-Zhao is a leading figure in the "middle way" philosophy in China. The "middle way" philosophy strives to avoid the extremes of nihilism and eternalism.

SENSE-OBJECT: The objects of our sensory faculties, such as color, form, sound, odor, flavor, and touch, and mental objects, such as feeling, perception, volition, and consciousness, are sense objects.

SENTIENT BEINGS: In Buddhism the term "sentient being" is used to define all beings able to have a conscious experience of feelings and perception.

SIXTH PATRIARCH: Sixth Patriarch Hui-Neng (638–713 BCE), regarded as the most important figure in Zen Buddhism, was instrumental in the wide propagation of Zen practice in China and later in Japan and Korea. All five schools of Zen Buddhism can trace their lineage to Hui-Neng. His teaching, as recorded in the Platform Sutra, is the most important sources of early Zen teaching.

SUCHNESS: The present reality as it is, beyond subjective explanation and interpretation is "suchness." It is sometimes translated as "thusness."

SURANGAMA SUTRA: One of the Buddhist texts frequently used in Zen teaching, the Surangama Sutra was translated to Chinese in 705 AD and is well known as a meditative study on the Void and the direct pointing out of the Mind. It also contains a description and analysis of twenty-five different methods for untying the mind from attachments and warnings of fifty false states of mind that one may encounter through spiritual practices.

SUTRA (AVATAMSAKA SUTRA): The Hua-Yen school of Buddhism teaches the simultaneity and totality of the manifestation of phenomena. It shows the integral relationship between phenomena and the ultimate principle, and the essential nondifference of phenomena.

SUTRA: Sutra are Buddhist scriptures that contain teachings of the Buddha.

TAO: Also referred to as "The Way," Tao refers to the principle that governs the functioning of the Mind and reality.

TAOISM: Taoism is a set of philosophical teachings and religious practices which originated in China and became an organized religion in the fifth century AD. The key text in Taoism is the *Tao Te Ching*. Taoists believe that man should live in harmony with nature through the Tao or "The Way," the idea of a great cosmic harmony. Taoist beliefs emphasize self-refinement, liberty and the pursuit of immortality.

TATHAGATA: *Tathagata* is a Sanskrit term frequently used by the Buddha to refer to himself, literally meaning "he who has come as he has gone." The term also can be understood as the two aspects of the Mind, the essence aspect that is the source and refuge of all phenomena, and the function aspect that is the presentation of reality.

TEN DIRECTIONS: Ten directions (of space) is a Buddhist cosmological concept including the north, south, east, west, up, down, northwest, northeast, southeast, and southwest.

THERAVADA: Literally, "teaching of the elder," Theravada is the oldest school of Buddhism. Presently, it is practiced predominantly in Sri Lanka and Southeast Asia.

THREE INSIGHTS OF ONE MIND: The Three Insights of One Mind show that emptiness, dependent designation (for example the conceptual labeling given to phenomena), and the middle way are the three aspects of non-duality, and therefore the complete penetration into non-duality through any one aspect will necessarily bring about the realization of the other aspects of non-duality. Furthermore it also means that it is actually not possible to realize any aspect of non-duality separately.

TRIPLE JEWELS: The Triple Jewels—the Buddha, the dharma and the sangha—are the points of refuge in Buddhism. In the literal sense, the word "Buddha" refers to the historical Buddha who left us with the dharma (or teaching), and the sangha represents the community of practitioners who apply the teaching in their practice and propagate the teaching to others. The Buddha, dharma and sangha also represent the awakening nature of the Mind, the universal principle that governs the manifestation of the Mind, and the pure functioning of the Mind. Because they represent the keys to liberation from all suffering and to attainment of eternal peace and joy, they are considered the most precious entities in this world, and are referred to as Jewels. Taking refuge in the Triple Jewels means that the practicioner accepts these three points of refuge as the ultimate guide of his spiritual life.

TUSITA HEAVEN: *Tusita* is a celestial plane of existence where a *bodhisattva* is reborn before appearing in this world as the Buddha.

VAIROCANA: The Vairocana Buddha is a historical Buddha whose name means "that which illuminates everything." Both the term and the Buddha refer to emptiness, or the essence of the Mind.

VAJRAYANA: Vajrayana, "the Diamond Vehicle," is also known as Tantric Buddhism. It is an extension of Mahayana Buddhism and similar in philosophical aspects, but because it incorporates additional esoteric techniques to achieve enlightenment, some practices can only be transmitted in person by a qualified, spiritual teacher under prescribed conditions.

VEXATION: Mental suffering that arises due to the gap between reality and our subjective perception of it is referred to as vexation.

WESTERN LAND OF BLISS: The Western Land of Bliss is the pure land of Amida Buddha. According to *Sutra*, Amida Buddha has forty-eight great vows that create an ideal learning environment for spiritual practitioners. Among these many marvelous wonders are: the ability to attend teachings given directly by Amida Buddha and travel to innumerable worlds of the Buddhas to receive teachings; trees and birds whose sounds and sights give dharma teaching without spoken words; and having an unlimited life span in which to deepen spiritual practice. Through the empowerment of Amida Buddha a practicioner is also able to take rebirth in other worlds for the sake of learning or helping other beings without the danger of regression to pitiful states of suffering and ignorance. This pure land is so particularly wonderful and free of all unpleasant aspects of worldly existence that it is also referred to as "The Land of Bliss."

**MASTER WU-MEN:** Master Wu-Men (1183–1260) is famous for compiling the Gateless Barrier, a collection of koan together with his own commentaries. He attained enlightenment through the practice of engaging the Huatou "Wu" (see Chao-Chou), therefore he is known as "Wu-Men" which literally means "no door (or gate)" or the door (or gate) of "Wu".

**MASTER XIANYAN:** In order to awaken the potential in him, Master Xian-Yan's teacher once asked him, "I am not interested in what you have learned or remembered from books and studies. Before you were born, before you distinguish what is east and west, from that place of your original self, now try to tell me something." Xian-Yan was speechless for a long time. Then he offered some words about his understanding of the Way, but the teacher disapproved of everything he said. Then Xian-Yan asked his teacher, "please explain the Way to me." His teacher said, "What I can say, is my own understanding. What benefit is there to flash it in front of your eyes?" Xian-Yan then returned to his quarter. Having poured through all the books and finding nothing to respond to the teacher, he said to himself, "hunger cannot be satisfied by drawing a cake." He burned up all the notes and books and said, "I shall forget about Buddhism for my whole life and simply be a traveling monk and rest the mind."

**POET XU DONG-PO:** (Su Dong-Po or Su-Shi) (1037–1101) is a major poet, artist, and calligrapher of the Song Dynasty. Having passed the civil service examination at the highest degree at the age of nineteen, he began a political career. Su was demoted and exiled several times due to philosophical differences with the central government's policies but was well-respected and loved by the people.

**MASTER XUEDOU:** This refers to Master Xuedou Zhongxian (980–1052). He compiled a collection of one hundred koans that later become the core of the Blue Cliff Record. One day Master Xuedou asked his teacher, Master Zhimen, "Without a single thought arising, why is there any fault?" Master Zhimen did not say a word but asked him to approach. Once Xuedou was close enough, Master Zhimen suddenly struck Xuedou's mouth with his whisk. Just before Xuedou had the chance to open his mouth and utter an argument, Master Zhimen struck him again. Right in that moment, Xuedou experienced enlightenment.

MASTER YONG-JIA (665–713): Master Yong-Jia is one of the five most prominent disciples of the Sixth Patriarch Hui-Neng and a scholar and practitioner of the Tian-Tai school's Shamatha-Vipassana (calm-abiding insight) meditation. Upon reading the Vimalakirti Nirdesa Sutra, he attained profound realization and was suggested by a friend to visit the Sixth Patriarch Hui-Neng to verify his understanding. When he met Master Hui-Neng, he circled the Sixth Patriarch three times and struck his staff on the ground. Hui-Neng said to him: "A monk must observe three thousand dignities and eighty thousand precepts in behavior. From where do you come with such arrogance?" Yong-Jia said, "Life and death is the utmost important matter; impermanence comes in a hurry." Hui-Neng said, "Why not realize the unborn and attain the unhurried?" Yong-Jia said, "The essence is originally unborn; realizing the source is without hurry." Hui-Neng said, "It is so, it is so." Yong-Jia then bowed and intended to depart immediately but Hui-Neng stopped him, "Departing so soon?" Yong-Jia replied, "The essence has not moved at all, how can there be any notion of soon?" Hui-Neng asked, "Who is the one that knows the unmoved?" Yong-Jia said, "That would be a distinction of your own making." Hui-Neng said, "You have quite profound realization of the meaning of the unborn." Yong-Jia said, "That which is unborn is not of meaning." Hui-Neng then asked, "Then who is making the distinction?" Yong-Jia said, "Even distinction is without meaning." Hui-Neng praised, "Excellent! Excellent! Please stay at least one night." Because of this famous encounter with the Sixth Patriarch, Master Yong-Jia is nicknamed "Overnight Awakening." One of his best-known writing is called the Yong-Jia's Song of the Realization of the Way.

MASTER ZHENJING KEWEN: Nicknamed Zhenjing, meaning "True Purity", Master Yunan Kewen (1025-1102) is of the Lin-Ji lineage. Before devoting himself to Zen, he was a famous scholar of both Confucianism and Hua-Yen and Mind-Only (Yogacara) schools of Buddhism. Once he visited a monastery and saw various statues depicting monks in postures of silent meditative concentration with closed eyes. He suddenly felt that everything he had learned before was much like the statues, although wonderful, they lack the vitality of life. Due to this realization, he gave up his scholarly pursuit and entered the path of Zen.